HUMAN RIGHTS AND THE INTERNET

HUMAN RIGHTS AND THE INTERNET

Joy Liddicoat

INTERSENTIA

Cambridge – Antwerp – Chicago

Intersentia Ltd
8 Wellington Mews
Wellington Street | Cambridge
CB1 1HW | United Kingdom
Tel: +44 1223 736 170
Email: mail@intersentia.co.uk
www.intersentia.com | www.intersentia.co.uk

Distribution for the UK and
Rest of the World (incl. Eastern Europe)
NBN International
1 Deltic Avenue, Rooksley
Milton Keynes MK13 8LD
United Kingdom
Tel: +44 1752 202 301 | Fax: +44 1752 202 331
Email: orders@nbninternational.com

Distribution for Europe
Lefebvre Sarrut Belgium NV
Hoogstraat 139/6
1000 Brussels
Belgium
Tel: +32 (0)800 39 067
Email: mail@intersentia.be

Distribution for the USA and Canada
Independent Publishers Group
Order Department
814 North Franklin Street
Chicago, IL 60610
USA
Tel: +1 800 888 4741 (toll free) | Fax: +1 312 337 5985
Email: orders@ipgbook.com

Human Rights and the Internet

Artwork on cover: Shutterstock

ISBN 978-1-83970-059-0
D/2021/7849/71
NUR 820

British Library Cataloguing in Publication Data. A catalogue record for this book is available from the British Library.

ACKNOWLEDGEMENTS

I want to thank the many people who made this book possible, including those I worked with at InternetNZ and the Association for Progressive Communications. When I joined InternetNZ in 2007, I thought I was joining a committee, but I found a community, a network, and a bunch of incredible mentors and new friends. Particular thanks to Jordan Carter, Ellen Strickland, Jamie Baddeley, Debbie Monahan, Richard Curry and Frank March. When I joined the Association for Progressive Communications in 2011, I took a job, but I found a purpose and lifetime inspiration. Thanks to all of the APC Network members and staff, in particular, Anriette Esterhuysen, Valeria Betancourt, Chat Garcia Ramilo and Karen Banks. With these organisations, I was able to experience the intellectual exhilaration of learning about the Internet, and the stress, pain, exhaustion, self-doubt and laughter of those who care about the Internet and human rights. This book is a tribute to everyone I worked with, and is dedicated to our continued shared struggle.

I am grateful to those who supported the initial idea for this book, including Anriette Esterhuysen, Dr Judy McGregor, Dr Marilyn Waring, Jane Foster, Alistair Farr, Dr Bill Germano, and my University of Otago colleagues John Zerilli, James Maclaurin, Alistair Knott, and Colin Gavaghan. Thanks to Jessica Palmer, Dean of the Law School at the University of Otago, for appointing me as a Research Affiliate as I commenced writing.

I am especially grateful to Dr Jeanne Snelling, my academic mentor, for her encouragement to write this book, her expertise in regulatory approaches to new technologies, and for providing a much-needed writing retreat. I am indebted to my brother, Richard Liddicoat, for reviewing drafts, talking me through the tough patches, and being a kind and critical muse. Thanks also to Rhian Gallagher, Marianne Quinn, and Susan Iversen of Karo Data Management, and to all the family, colleagues and friends who listened and encouraged me over emails, online meetings, cups of coffee, lunches, walks and talks – you know who you are. I am also grateful to all those at Intersentia, in particular Ann-Christin Maak-Scherpe, for kind and professional assistance, and Rebecca Moffat – an amazing editor.

Finally, thanks to my partner, Jo Fox, for her unwavering support: without you, my human rights work and this book would not have been possible.

CONTENTS

INTRODUCTION

This book is for anyone who is curious about the Internet and how it relates to the world around them, and to human rights. Curiosity can be both rewarding and punishing. Even a brief look at the news can lead to the conclusion that the Internet is out of control: some kind of wild, dangerous world where there are no rules and no place for human rights. Yet, like our human rights, which are universal, the Internet was designed to be for everyone, everywhere. This book is a story of how these two separate things, our human rights and the Internet, became inextricably linked. I offer it now, with all its imperfections, because I know that the remarkable successes of Internet and human rights communities were not achieved by chance. This book is for those who are curious about how this process happened, and where it might lead: Internet users, civil society organisations, policymakers, business or technical experts and lawyers.

This book is not written exclusively for lawyers. However, as a human rights lawyer, I know that the history and accomplishments of human rights are, rightly, the subject of fierce debate. For all its high moral promise, the international human rights system is fraught with imperfections. Some commentators, such as Makay Mutua[1] or Samuel Moyn,[2] question whether the time of human rights is over; if, indeed, it ever really began. It is impossible to deny, and equally impossible to do full justice to, these contested views in the short space of this book. But this book is not a philosophical treatise on the theoretical meaning of law, or a technical jurisprudential academic analysis. My goal is more pragmatic: to tell some of the story of the evolution of the Internet and human rights.

For now, then, all I can do is acknowledge that, for some people at least, the legitimacy of human rights is not well-settled, and that these

1 M. MUTUA, 'Is the Age of Human Rights Over?' in S. A. McCLENNEN and A. S. MOORE (eds.), *Routledge Companion to Literature and Human Rights*, Routledge, London and New York 2016, pp. 450–58.

2 S. MOYN, *Not Enough: Human Rights in an Unequal World*. Harvard University Press, Cambridge 2018.

contested views influence discussion about human rights today, including the struggle to have human rights recognised in our online lives. Is the Internet the ultimate expression of human freedom, without government, rules or borders? Or is the Internet a public place where the human rights of everyone must be respected and protected?

While it took me some time to work out these complexities, those I worked with (whether from civil society, academia, government, or technical communities) understood all too well the conceptual contradictions, legal limitations and political complexities of both the Internet and the international human rights system. There was no road map for developing human rights online, so this book simply charts twelve years of my experience with the Internet and human rights, including time spent working with activists, policymakers and technical experts.

Looking back – to paraphrase an Irish saying – if we had wanted to get where we were going, we wouldn't have started from there. But, in the late 2000s, there we were: in the midst of a complex, contested, contradictory, at times wholly unsatisfactory legal, technical and highly political situation. The messy reality of struggling to understand, and then advocate for, human rights online in the early part of the twenty-first century is, therefore, where I will start: where I *must* start.

This book has two parts: Part I charts the history of human rights online, while Part II canvasses some of the new challenges of the digital age. Starting with these two separate subjects – the Internet and human rights – Chapter 1 outlines how the Internet works, the technical standards that govern its operation, and the network of Internet communities that developed, and which continue to keep the Internet operating. After a brief outline of the principles underlying the Internet, the chapter recalls some of the early promise of the Internet. Next, the international human rights system is introduced, with a brief outline of how this works, and the underlying principles that keep the system operating. The chapter presents some preliminary analysis of how these two systems were interacting by the end of 2010, with examples of how different uses of the Internet came to challenge fundamental ideas about human rights. Finally, the chapter introduces two themes that will be explored throughout the book: the concept of Internet governance, and the diverse collaborations and communities that emerged to create, maintain and develop new technologies.

Chapter 2 explores why human rights matter in an Internet context, introducing Internet activists and their experiences of interference with Internet access and use. Some of these interferences appeared similar to old, offline human rights interferences, such as jamming radio or television signals or restricting access to information, but some were entirely new and specific to the Internet, raising questions about Internet-related rights. The chapter discusses several examples, culminating in a detailed study of the Internet shutdown in Egypt in early 2011, and the debate about whether this was a human rights violation.

Chapter 3 has a theoretical focus, setting out some of the historical conceptual challenges to defining human rights violations on the Internet. The chapter explores whether interference with the Internet can be a human rights violation, by examining the definition of such a violation. Using a broad, three-step definition (a clearly defined right with a rights-holder and a duty-bearer, an interference with the right that results in harm, and a remedy), the chapter examines the conceptual challenges of applying each part of the definition to the Internet, providing examples of why these have caused problems. In defining rights-holders and duty-bearers, the chapter examines the case of the right to be forgotten. In defining harm on the Internet, women's human rights defenders' advocacy for recognition of technology-based violence against women is also discussed. The chapter then discusses the difficulties in identifying and quantifying appropriate remedies. The chapter concludes with a brief discussion of the governance implications of these conceptual challenges, including the challenges of determining who was in control of Internet-related human rights violations, and who, therefore, should be held accountable.

Chapter 4 charts the strategies of those advocating for human rights, in light of these conceptual difficulties, through the lens of my work with the Association for Progressive Communications. The chapter briefly outlines the development of communication rights and the rise of Internet rights and principles, as concepts, as well as the use of the rights-based approach to interferences with the Internet. The challenges for governments and policymakers are discussed, including a brief overview of regulatory approaches to the Internet. The chapter discusses the effectiveness of advocacy for communication rights, and the move towards advocacy for Internet rights. Observing the lack of any substantive discussion about the Internet and human rights in the international human rights system, the chapter concludes with a case study on developing an advocacy strategy, the Connect Your Rights campaign, for the United Nations Human Rights Council (UNHRC). This strategy focussed on the work of the UN Special Rapporteur on the Right to Freedom of Opinion and Expression.

Chapter 5 explores how the concept of human rights online formally emerged within the UNHRC. The chapter outlines how advocacy for freedom of expression and freedom of the Internet, by civil society groups and governments alike, helped to bring the Internet into the mainstream of the international human rights system. Through a series of careful, well-planned steps, new standards began to emerge that would resolve some of the conceptual difficulties, and crystallise the definition of an Internet-related human rights violation. The chapter follows these steps through the annual report of the Special Rapporteur, to the Expert Panel on Freedom of Expression and the Internet, and on to the Universal Periodic Review process. The chapter examines the historic UNHRC resolution that affirmed that 'offline' human rights must also apply online, and concludes by briefly canvassing the implications, for Internet governance, of these developments.

Part II examines some of the challenges for human rights online, in the digital era. Chapter 6 examines the revelations of global mass Internet surveillance and the wider effects that these have had on technical and civil society communities working on Internet governance. The chapter outlines how the revelations led to new collaborations between human rights, Internet rights organisations, and those working to navigate conceptual challenges and tensions between the openness and freedom of the Internet and accountability for human rights violations. A case study of the right to privacy illustrates the emergence of human rights in the digital age, signalling a conceptual move beyond Internet rights, and a more fundamental transformation to the concept of human rights online in the digital age. The chapter concludes with observations about the emergence of 'human rights online', and the technical community's response.

Chapter 7 examines human rights and the Internet in the time of Covid-19. After a brief overview of the outbreak of the global pandemic, the chapter takes a more in-depth look at three types of digital contact-tracing technologies, and the human rights issues that they raise. The chapter concludes with a brief outline of some new digital proximity tracing laws that are designed to protect human rights, and reflects on the limits of technological approaches to the pandemic. In so doing, it examines the prospects and challenges for human rights online, marking both significant progress and a sharp reminder of the limits of technology and the need to ensure protection and promotion of human rights online *and* offline.

Finally, Chapter 8 examines the challenge of artificial intelligence (AI), in order to demonstrate how much technology, and concepts of human rights, have developed in the last ten years. The chapter gives a brief summary of the field of narrow AI and machine learning tools, and outlines some human rights implications of algorithms and AI tools, including bias and discrimination, transparency and due process, and fairness. In doing so, it aims to show that new collaborations are forming between human rights defenders, ethicists, engineers, researchers, developers and other technology workers and communities. Like their predecessors in the early days of the Internet and human rights, these collaborations are helping to expose human rights concerns, and to respond collectively to the regulatory and other challenges of these new technologies. The chapter presents a case study at the intersection of human rights, algorithms and social media: the Christchurch Call, a multi-stakeholder initiative in response to terrorist attacks on two mosques in Christchurch, New Zealand, in March 2019.

The book concludes with a summary of the preceding chapters, some reflections on regulatory approaches, and a look ahead at some of the new, emerging issues that will confront human rights in the digital age, such as the spatial Internet.

'Human rights online' can be a confusing concept and term. In this book, I have attempted, among other things, to chart the rise of this term from the concept of communication rights, to Internet rights, then to human rights online and, ultimately, to human rights in the digital age. Like the development of any new concept, the process is not linear, and owes its progress to many hundreds or thousands of activists, academics, regulators, policymakers and others who have striven to articulate their changing world, not in theoretical terms, but in the realities of daily life. Throughout this book, I have endeavoured to tell their stories: to highlight the reality of human rights and the Internet. My goal was to keep these stories as accurate as possible but, in some cases, I have changed the location or other identifying details to protect the identity of individual human rights defenders. While I have drawn on my own experiences, I have generally cited publicly-available research for all my case studies. Ultimately, this is my story, with all its fallibility and foibles, so I apologise in advance for any errors, which will be entirely my own. I hope that this book makes some small contribution towards understanding how the field of human rights online developed within the international human rights system.

PART I
HUMAN RIGHTS ONLINE

CHAPTER 1

THE INTERNET AND HUMAN RIGHTS

A Tale of Two Systems

1. INTRODUCTION

At the heart of the Internet is an incredible community, and a story of how an extraordinary resource was created and then freely given away. Likewise, at the heart of human rights, there are incredible individuals and communities who have overcome enormous odds to inspire the world. This chapter introduces both. Firstly, it will discuss the Internet, some key technical standards that enable its operation, and some of the important communities who keep the Internet going; then the chapter will give a brief outline of how the international human rights system works, along with a description of the communities who work within it. These two systems have similarities and differences which, as we shall soon see, created tensions – and synergies – as they converged, leading to entirely new ideas such as Internet governance. Within just a few years of its creation, Internet users were challenging fundamental ideas about human rights, and human rights were challenging the very essence of the Internet.

2. HOW DOES THE INTERNET WORK?

As individual users, we can happily use the Internet while being entirely unaware of its complex ecosystem. So many of our daily tasks, such as sending and receiving email, reading news, conducting research, chatting with family and friends and watching movies, are done in this way. But to understand our human rights online, it is helpful to know a little of the basics about how the Internet works. There are many resources and guides about the Internet, and I am a lawyer, not a technical expert, so what follows is a simplified outline.

There is no international treaty governing the operation of the Internet; no single law or legal framework, no 'government' of the Internet. Instead, a loose community of individuals and groups (the 'technical community') operate open and standardised technical protocols which, when adopted, allow the Internet to function.[1] However, the Internet ecosystem is much wider than this community, and encompasses telecommunications networks, network operators, government regulatory policy (such as that on competitive access to broadband), Internet service providers, platform providers (such as YouTube and Facebook), and many other elements.[2]

To understand how the Internet works, we must put aside any idea that the Internet is like the telephone, radio waves or satellite broadcasts. The Internet does not operate through a continuous signal on a single channel, like a television broadcast, nor a direct line, like the telephone. Instead, the Internet operates to transfer information (for example, an email) from one computer to another by dividing this information into many small packets of data. It transmits each packet from a computer at one end, or edge, of the network, to another computer at the other end, via a network that distributes and reassembles the packets into the information transmitted, when they are received by another computer.[3] These data packets are designed to travel freely through the network. To enable this, the network is designed to be neutral, carrying all data, without discrimination, from one end point of the network to another. The basic underlying concept of the Internet, then, is simply a large network of computers connected to each other, sending and receiving tiny packets of data across a decentralised network.

This travel happens though routers, which help packets of data find the right 'route' to their destination as they travel over the network from one computer to another. In order for the data to 'know' where to go, each stop along the way needs its own unique address, much like the address needed to send a letter. On the Internet, these addresses have a unique number – for example, 192.168.1.100 – known as an Internet Protocol (IP)

---

1 B. M. LEINER et al, 'A Brief History of the Internet' (1997) the Internet Society <https://www.internetsociety.org/internet/history-internet/brief-history-internet/> accessed 06.05.2020.

2 See the Internet Society <http://www.isoc.org/Internet/issues/ecosystem.shtml> accessed 08.08.2020.

3 A. DORIA, 'Internet Technology and Networks' in D. SOUTER (ed.), *APC ICT Policy Handbook*, 2nd ed., Association for Progressive Communications, 2009, pp. 113–20, p. 113.

address.[4] Every end point on the Internet – every device that connects to it – will have its own unique IP address: your laptop, PC, smartphone, or even a smart appliance like a television or refrigerator that is connected to the Internet.[5] You can find your own IP address simply by typing 'what's my IP address?' into any browser on your computer or other device.

The Internet works as a complete network because it uses open standards, like Internet Protocols, that allow computers to connect to each other and find routes for packets of data. As the data travels, and when it reaches its end point, a three-way 'handshake' takes place, whereby the request to send and receive information is verified and, once verified, transfer of the data takes place.[6]

In order for this to work, each computer connection requires a stack of such protocols, and each stack has several layers upon which other applications can be built. Say, for example, you want to go to a website. The protocol stack that enables you to browse websites might have four layers: the hardware layer (that converts binary data packets to network signals and back, such as on cables or modems); an Internet Protocol layer (that directs packets of data to specific IP addresses); a Transmission Control Protocol layer (which directs packets to a specific application on a computer using a numbered port); and an application protocols layer (which direct packets to specific applications such as the World Wide Web or email).[7]

Today, protocol stacks are built into all computers so that they can connect with other computers, although it wasn't always this way. There are many types of application protocol, but some of the more well-known ones are the Hypertext Transfer Protocol (HTTP) and its secure extension (HTTPS), the World Wide Web protocol (WWW), and the Simple Mail Transfer Protocol (SMTP).[8]

---

4 J. POSTEL (ed.), 'The Internet Protocol', RFC 791, Information Sciences Institute, California, September 1981.

5 For an excellent discussion of the rise of connected appliances and the 'Internet of Things', see J. ZITTRAIN, *The Future of the Internet and How to Stop It*, Yale University Press, New Haven 2008.

6 J. POSTEL (ed.), 'The Transmission Control Protocol', RFC 793, Information Sciences Institute, California, September 1981.

7 In the early 1990s, Peter Tattam, an Australian academic with no formal computer training, developed a programme called Trumpet Winsock, which enabled users of PCs running Microsoft Windows to connect with other users also running Microsoft Windows: see J. ZITTRAIN, above n. 5, pp. 29–30.

8 Tim Berners-Lee coined the phrase 'the World Wide Web,' creating, among other things, a programming language with hypertext link capability (Hypertext Markup

Each website has a unique IP address – that long number mentioned above – because it represents one stop, or edge point, on the Internet. There are hundreds of millions of websites, and not many of us have the ability to remember the long strings of numbers that make up IP addresses. Accordingly, to help make IP addresses easier for humans to remember, the Internet community, led by Jon Postel, developed the Domain Name System (DNS), a protocol for identifying computers by name rather than number, for example www.intersentia.com.[9] The protocols for domain names divide these into levels, designed to be read from left to right. Top-level domains (TLDs) have two categories: country specific (ccTLDs – for example, the New Zealand country specific code is '.nz'), and generic (gTLDs – for example, '.org').[10] Related protocols guide the rules on who can register names in each domain, and the roles and responsibilities of the person or organisation that manages the domain, or the domain system, in which their TLD operates.[11] Apart from being easier to remember, names also make it easier to 'move' on the Internet, because changing a name is much simpler than changing an IP address, requiring only that numbers be redirected to a single name, much like redirecting the post when you move house.[12]

When he developed the DNS, Postel used a rough taxonomy of 13 sorts of sector that he thought might use domain names, such as commercial companies ('.com'), organisations ('.org'), militaries ('.mil'), governments ('.gov'), and educational institutions ('.edu'). As demand for these domains started to increase in the 1990s, responsibility for managing them was delegated to various individuals around the world: people scattered in universities, telecommunications companies and elsewhere.[13]

Language or HTML), which became the primary publishing format for the Web; see the World Wide Web Consortium <https://www.w3.org/Consortium/facts> accessed 22.06.2020.

9 C. REED, *Computer Law: The Law and Regulation of Information Technology*, 7th ed., Oxford University Press, Oxford 2011, pp. 544–46.

10 ibid., p. 545.

11 Internet Assigned Numbers Authority <www.iana.org> accessed 04.06.2019. The official list of all TLDs is maintained by the Internet Assigned Number Authority, which is the global coordinator of the root zone files, IP addressing and other Internet resource protocols.

12 M. L. MUELLER, *Ruling the Root: Internet Governance and the Taming of Cyberspace*, MIT Press, Cambridge, MA 2001, p. 40.

13 InterNIC was the original source of public information about Internet domain name services, a role now coordinated by the Internet Corporation for Assigned Names and Numbers (ICANN). The InterNIC archival website is still available <https://www.internic.net/faqs/authoritative-dns.html> accessed 22.06.2020.

Today, there are more than 400 TLDs (including nearly 200 ccTLDs). The Internet Corporation for Assigned Names and Numbers (ICANN) has responsibility for global coordination of the communities that develop standards for the DNS, and assigns blocks of the many billions of available IP addresses to one of the five regional Internet registries for allocation within their respective regions.[14]

Each organisation that manages a domain name space must provide 'name server' computers to support the domain. These are computers that store lists of domain names and associated IP addresses, and other data (such as the names and addresses of people who register domain names) about a subset (or zone) of the name space.[15] The most complete and authoritative resource record of information for a domain is the otherwise-unnamed root zone file. The root zone file is supported by root name servers which use information in resource records about domain name registrations to resolve queries about IP addresses.[16] Finally, for all of this to work, it is vital that no two domain names are identical. To ensure this, most domain name registries operate name registration at the highest level of a TLD on a first come, first served basis.[17]

In 1985, the Internet was a well-established technology within some sectors of society, supporting a community of developers and researchers, with a few other groups just starting to use it for email communications.[18] However, by the mid-1990s, Internet infrastructure had rapidly developed to include shared Internet exchange points that were set up across the globe, guided by an 'acceptable use policy' ensuring that these exchange points could only be used for research and education purposes. The effect was to create commercial opportunities for the use of the data packets (or 'traffic') on exchange points, not the exchange points themselves.

The reality of this complex system was brought home to me on a visit to the European Centre for Nuclear Research (CERN) in 2012.[19] I was

---

14 Internet Corporation for Assigned Names and Numbers <www.icann.org> accessed 22.06.2020.

15 M. L. MUELLER, above n. 12, pp. 43–45. The Registration Data Access Protocol (RDAP) is expected to eventually replace the current WHOIS protocol, which relates to personal information about the registrant of a domain name and those authorised to access that information (see: <https://www.icann.org/resources/pages/rdap-faqs-2018-08-31-en> accessed 09.11.2020).

16 ibid.

17 ibid.

18 B. M. LEINER et al, above n. 1.

19 For information about CERN, see: <https://home.cern/science/computing/birth-web> and <http://line-mode.cern.ch/> accessed 22.06.2020.

attending an ICANN meeting in Geneva, and the Internet Society invited a few of us to visit the nearby European regional Internet exchange point: the computers through which all the data packets (the Internet traffic) in Europe passed. It was an unusual thing for a lawyer to do, but I could not resist the opportunity to go to the place that exemplified the cooperative nature of the technical community, and the place where British scientist Tim Berners-Lee had invented the World Wide Web.

Today, CERN is home to complex science projects such as the Large Hadron Collider, but in 1989 Berners-Lee was working with Robert Cailliau on how to create software that would easily find the millions of documents scattered on different computers throughout the Internet. This involved creating auto-indexing software, and developing the Internet's first browser, followed soon after by a browser that could work on many different kinds of computer. The software included the development of a World Wide Web page with an address known as a Uniform Resource Locator, or URL, which simply points to where on the network a particular resource (such as a document) could be found. The result was to transform machine-readable language into human-readable language, in much the same way as the DNS was doing for IP addresses.

As the technology began to be picked up by others, Berners-Lee and Cailliau decided to release the software into the public domain with an open licence, with the immediate effect that no one could own the World Wide Web. From that moment, the Web belonged to all of us.

The technical community was building global resources like regional Internet exchange points, and giving open access for non-commercial purposes.[20] This openness is a hallmark of the Internet community. Unlike other entities that might own and operate telecommunications, broadcast or satellite infrastructure for profit, the Internet is, at its core, designed to be a global resource. The Internet is not 'owned' by anyone, and relies upon the multi-stakeholder nature of the Internet community to create standards in a variety of ways.

I remember vividly the people who led my early introduction into the Internet: Avri Doria, Frank March, Debbie Monahan, Andy Linton, Jac sm Kee, Keith Davidson, and many others. These people were mainly technical experts, but their deep passion for the Internet, and strongly held beliefs that it should be open and free from capture, struck me just

---

20 Packet Clearing House (PCH) is the international organisation responsible for providing operational support to critical Internet infrastructure such as the Internet exchange points <https://www.pch.net/> accessed 22.06.2020.

as much as their technical expertise. I learned that such beliefs among the 'technical community', and the values underpinning them, are etched into the most basic operating principles of Internet standards-making processes.

Of all the 'founding beliefs' about the Internet that were impressed upon me (such as the end-to-end, decentralised nature of the network, and the free flow of data packets), two seemed especially important to almost all of the technical community members I met. Firstly, the belief in 'rough consensus and running code', which, so far as I could tell, broadly translated into collaborative decision-making and practical experiences help develop the best standards.[21] Secondly, the belief that you should be 'conservative in what you send, and liberal in what you accept'.[22]

The Internet Engineering Task Force (IETF), for example, which coordinates Internet standards-making, has a straightforward mission: 'to make the Internet work better'.[23] From humble beginnings, the IETF now has participants from the spheres of government, civil society, academia, research and industry (including network operators and vendors). The IETF operates as a meritocracy: participants are 'generally concerned with finding the best technical solutions to issues of the day and place high value on a set of technological principles, rather than institutional allegiance'.[24] This idea will be explored in more detail in Chapter 4, but for now it is important to understand that 'multi-stakeholder' rather than single-stakeholder rule-making was an important founding concept of the Internet.

Today, there are three primary organisations that keep the Internet running: the IETF, the Internet Architecture Board (IAB)[25] and ICANN. Each, to one extent or another, espouses these principles of working as a meritocracy, with multiple stakeholders of equal status working for the best technical solutions to keep the Internet working and improving.

---

21 The IETF Trust, 'How We Work' <https://www.ietf.org/how/runningcode/> accessed 30.06.2020. See also H. ALVESTRAND (ed.) 'A Mission Statement for the IETF' RFC 3935, the Internet Society, Norway, October 2004.

22 The IETF Trust, 'The Tao of the IETF' 2019 <https://www.ietf.org/about/participate/tao/> accessed 05.05.2020.

23 H. ALVESTRAND, above n. 21 and see also P. HOFFMAN and S. BRADNER, 'Defining the IETF' RFC 3233, the Internet Society, Cambridge, MA 2002.

24 J. LIDDICOAT and A. DORIA 'Human Rights and Internet Protocols: Comparing Processes and Principles' (2012) the Internet Society, p. 2 <https://www.internetsociety.org/wp-content/uploads/2017/08/Human20Rights20and20Internet20Protocols-20Comparing20Processes20and20Principles.pdf> accessed 15.03.2021.

25 The IAB provides 'long range technical direction for Internet development'; see <https://www.iab.org/> accessed 22.06.2020.

There might seem a lot to absorb, but rest assured that you do not need to know how all of these protocols work, or what all of these organisations do, to understand human rights online. In fact, most of these organisations would prefer to stay out of the limelight altogether and let you get on with using the Internet, blithely unaware of their existence, and without worrying about their technical issues. But, for now, what is important to grasp is that the Internet works because of the many protocols which people have voluntarily agreed to use, and around which a global network for free flow of information across millions of computers has developed.

To summarise how the Internet works, it operates as a distributed computer network with packets of data at the edges of the network finding routes across the network to their end destinations: packets of data that interact with stacks of protocols that create layers upon which other applications can be built. Packets of data travel freely, and routers direct these packets where they need to go. The Internet works because all computers, and the people who build and use them, agree to share the same protocols: protocols developed collaboratively by a diverse, multi-stakeholder community. This community, and its underlying belief in an end-to-end, decentralised network focused on empowering those at the edges, rather than the centre, of its architecture – of free open access to infrastructure, and of rules or standards based on the best ideas – this is the heart and lifeblood of the Internet.

As we will see, a failure to grasp these basic concepts, and a desire to regulate the Internet and the actions of the technical community in the same way as previous technologies, resulted in tensions between groups and caused many problems. But, before we explore these tensions and problems, we also need to understand a bit about how the international human rights system works.

3. HOW DO INTERNATIONAL HUMAN RIGHTS WORK?

Like the Internet, the modern foundations of international human rights developed in the later part of the twentieth century. Technical descriptions of human rights focus on the rule of law, constitutional documents, national laws and international treaties. The detail of these descriptions is, of course, necessary for understanding how the technical aspects of human rights work in practice. However, just as technical descriptions of the Internet do not convey its whole ecosystem, such technical descriptions do not adequately explain how human rights cohere into a single unifying concept. What follows, then, is a basic overview of human rights, the international human rights system, and how international human rights standards are made, together with a brief commentary on the concepts holding the system together.

The evolution of human rights principles has been traced across many centuries in all regions of the world, in various forms.[26] For our purposes, the starting point for global, rather than national, human rights standards was the aftermath of World War II. The United Nations (UN) was created in 1945, and the founding Charter set out its basic purpose:[27]

> To achieve international co-operation in solving international problems of an economic, social, cultural, or humanitarian character, and in promoting and encouraging respect for human rights and for fundamental freedoms for all without distinction as to race, sex, language, or religion.

The Charter did not define 'human rights and fundamental freedoms'. That came in 1948, when members of the UN ('Member States') drafted the Universal Declaration of Human Rights (UDHR). This provided, for the first time in the UN, a clear, agreed statement about human rights:[28]

> All human beings are born free and equal in dignity and rights. They are endowed with reason and conscience and should act towards one another in a spirit of brotherhood.

The UDHR set out a remarkably abiding list of human rights and freedoms, including: freedom from discrimination; the right to life, liberty and security; freedom of expression and of association; the right to legal remedies; freedom from arbitrary arrest and detention; the right to privacy; freedom of thought, conscience, and religion; the right to take

---

26 M. HASS, *International Human Rights: A Comprehensive Introduction*, Routledge, London 2014, Chapter 1: 'The Nature and History of Human Rights', pp. 10–18; and, e.g. A. SEN, 'Human Rights and Asian Values' (16th Morgenthau Memorial Lecture on Ethics and Foreign Policy), Carnegie Council on Ethics and International Affairs, New York, 1997.

27 Charter of the United Nations (1945), Article 1(3).

28 Universal Declaration of Human Rights (1948), Article 1.

part in government; rights to social security, work, education, adequate housing; the right to a family and cultural life; and the right to share in the benefits of scientific advancement.

The Declaration affirmed that human rights are universal, inalienable and interconnected. In much the same way that Internet Protocols derive their authority from community adoption, the UDHR draws its strong moral authority from the overwhelming number of states that have adopted it, as they must do in order to become members of the UN.[29] Two more detailed standards were developed later: one on civil and political rights (like the right to vote, freedom of expression, freedom of association, and the right to a fair trial),[30] and one on economic, cultural and social rights (like the rights to health, education, an adequate standard of living, and to social security).[31] Together with the UDHR, these are known as the International Bill of Human Rights.[32]

Gradually, other international human rights standards followed: the Convention against Torture and Other Cruel, Inhuman or Degrading Treatment or Punishment (UNCAT), the International Convention on the Elimination of All Forms of Racial Discrimination (ICERD), the Convention on the Elimination of All Forms of Discrimination Against Women (CEDAW), the Convention on the Rights of the Child (UNCROC), and the Convention on the Rights of Persons with Disabilities (CRPD). There is a great deal of literature on these standards, as well as more recent standards such as the Declaration of the Rights of Indigenous Peoples (UNDRIP).These various rights and freedoms are sometimes referred to as first, second or third-generation rights, a term coined by Karel Vašák to categorise the development of civil and political rights. First-generation rights are those which developed before the twentieth century, in contrast to the second generation of economic, cultural and social rights which developed after World War II, and third-generation rights to development and self-determination.[33] New issues, such as communication and digital

---

29 For this reason, also, the Governmental Advisory Committee to ICANN refers to the Universal Declaration of Human Rights; see, e.g. ICANN, 'GAC Principles Regarding New gTLDs', 28 March 2007, Clause 2.1(a) <https://gac.icann.org/contentMigrated/gac-principles-regarding-new-gtlds> accessed 03.03.2021.

30 The International Covenant on Civil and Political Rights (1966).

31 International Covenant on Economic, Social and Cultural Rights (1976).

32 Office of the High Commissioner for Human Rights, 'The International Bill of Human Rights' (1996), Fact Sheet No. 2 (Rev. 1), United Nations, Geneva <https://www.ohchr.org/Documents/Publications/FactSheet2Rev.1en.pdf> accessed 03.03.2021.

33 K. VAŠÁK, 'Human Rights: A Thirty-Year Struggle: the Sustained Efforts to give Force of Law to the Universal Declaration of Human Rights', [1977] *UNESCO Courier* 30:11.

rights, discussed in more detail in Chapter 5, have been called fourth-generation rights.[34]

For now, the main point to keep in mind is that the UN Charter and the International Bill of Rights established the basic framework of the international human rights system: governments became duty-bearers, charged with the responsibility to act as guardians or stewards in protecting the human rights and freedoms of their peoples. That responsibility is often expressed as a government's duty to:

- *respect* rights and freedoms (for example, uphold the rule of law, refrain from arbitrary or unreasonable arrest or detention, ensure due process and fair trial, not interfere with rights such as privacy and freedom of religion);
- *protect* rights and freedoms (for example, protect citizens from violation of their rights to life, liberty and security by others, provide remedies where rights are violated); and
- *promote* rights and freedoms (so that people are aware of their rights and know how to exercise them).

As guardians of their own citizens' human rights, national governments submitted to the governments of other UN Member States monitoring their human rights performance (essentially through a complex system of mutual review and peer pressure). The international human rights system works, fundamentally, because it is based on the three simple principles outlined above, and seeks to use the rule of law, not force or war, to uphold them. The basic principles have remained constant as new standards have developed through negotiation and been adopted through an 'opt-in' process, coming into force when sufficient numbers of Member States agree.[35]

In a similar way to the organisations that make up the core of the Internet standards-making bodies, there are three pillars to the international human rights system: the United Nations Human Rights Council (HRC), treaty bodies, and Special Procedures. The HRC sits at the apex of this system, headed by a High Commissioner for Human Rights, appointed

---

[34] C. SOH, D. CONNOLLY and S. NAM, 'Time for a Fourth Generation of Human Rights?', UNRISD, 01.03.2018 <http://www.unrisd.org/TechAndHumanRights-Soh-et-al> accessed 22.06.2020.

[35] The number of signatories required varies widely and, in each case, is also negotiated. For example, 35 countries were needed for the ICCPR to come into force, 25 for ICERD, and 20 for UNCAT.

on a rotational basis by governments. The Council sits three times a year, receiving updates from countries, and overseeing a wide programme of human rights reporting. The Special Procedures are individuals appointed in relation to specific topics, such as freedom of expression, violence against women, or racism, or to monitor a particular situation or country. The treaty bodies are responsible for overseeing reports on specific treaties or conventions, such as those relating to civil and political rights, or discrimination against women and girls.[36]

When it comes to disputes between national governments, the UN does not generally see litigation as the appropriate way to seek remedies or accountability between nations (and, in any case, there is no appropriate international court system). Instead, when the UDHR was being negotiated in the 1940s, governments agreed to establish new international forums, like the HRC, as places for accountability.

Accountability to these forums is primarily by way of reporting. For example, once a state ratifies a treaty (such as the International Covenant on Civil and Political Rights (ICCPR)), it agrees to report periodically on domestic implementation. Some treaties have also adopted complaint procedures (known as optional protocols) which individuals can use to make complaints about their country to the UN. Each treaty has different standards for accountability. For example, states are obliged to implement economic, cultural and social rights as resources allow, through a system known as 'progressive realisation'. Civil and political rights, on the other hand, must be implemented immediately; some, such as freedom from torture, can never be suspended or limited, even in emergencies.

The premise underlying these forms of accountability is that states, as equal members of the international community of nations, agree to subject their conduct to the scrutiny of other states. In so doing, states also agree to abide by recommendations, or take into account observations made, about matters within their own borders. States, therefore, agree to be publicly accountable for their human rights performance. In practice, things are quite different. UN membership is restricted to 'Member States' – governments of one form or another – and its operations are inherently political.[37] UN human rights processes rely on consensus, because each

---

36 V. MANHIRE (ed.), *The United Nations Handbook 2019–2020*, Ministry of Foreign Affairs and Trade, New Zealand 2019.

37 The Charter of the United Nations sets out the UN's basic operating principles, including membership and broad rules for participation. One significant exception

country retains autonomy over matters within its own borders. Some refuse, for various reasons, to sign up to even the more basic human rights standards and, under UN rules, are free to do so.[38] However, when enough states sign a human rights standard, it comes into force.[39] Some standards take many years to come into force.[40]

Businesses and the private sector generally sit outside the international human rights system. International human rights standards-making is an intergovernmental process which is multi-layered, and premised on legitimacy through negotiation, adoption and use; it also includes various mechanisms for oversight and accountability. The basic process is government-led, with other actors only able to participate if approved as registered civil society groups, and subject to strict conditions. However, civil society groups play a critical role in bringing human rights violations to the attention of the international human rights bodies (for example, through their own monitoring of government activities or other reporting).

At the national level, the international human rights standards are expected to be taken into account, but it is up to each country to determine how best to do so. Some countries expressly incorporate international standards into their domestic law, others by implication, others not at all. Some consider the international standards to be binding, others as more or less a persuasive aid to interpreting national laws; still others consider them irrelevant. National practices vary widely, even among courts, and include the development of new constitutions (or amendments to existing ones), legislation, case law and various other instruments that set out national human rights standards. Since most countries already have their own laws and legal systems, processes for public participation, and for taking human rights cases, vary as widely as forms of national governance. National civil society groups and their global counterparts, such as Human Rights Watch and Amnesty International, also play a critical role in these processes.

---

from membership is the Vatican City, which has never ratified the UN Charter, and remains an observer State.

38 For example, a few countries (the US, Iran, Somalia, Sudan, Tonga, Palau and Nauru) have not yet ratified the CEDAW <https://www.un.org/womenwatch/daw/cedaw/states.htm> accessed 22.06.2020.

39 When signing on to a treaty, some states may elect to attach 'reservations', exempting themselves from adherence to certain clauses in the standards.

40 For example, although the ICCPR was negotiated and signed in 1966, it did not come into force until 1976, when the last of the required 35 countries ratified it.

Finally, there are some particular concepts that underpin the general legal definitions of human rights:

- 'Positive' and 'negative' rights: a positive right is one that requires a government to take action to ensure that it is always upheld (such as taking action to prevent discrimination); a negative right is one that should not be interfered with – it requires no action. One example is non-interference with privacy.
- Rights and freedoms can be limited – they are not 'absolute' – but limitations must be fair and reasonable, and imposed only through a lawful process (such as a court order or valid law) or, in exceptional and time-limited situations, such as a national or other emergency.

The international human rights system is complex, but the key concepts are: human rights are universal (the birthright of all people everywhere); and human rights are not absolute, and can be limited in certain circumstances. The international human rights system is designed to protect human rights by recognising the right of states to govern, and the duties of states to respect, protect and promote the human rights of their citizens. As these are duties owed by governments to their citizens, the private sector generally sits outside the system. Standards are agreed through intergovernmental processes premised on legitimacy through negotiation, adoption, and use; and there are various peer-to-peer mechanisms for oversight and accountability.

The global transformation of human rights, from moral or philosophical imperatives into a framework of legally recognised rights and freedoms shared between nations, is an ongoing process. But the basic framework described above has been reaffirmed by UN members;[41] it was the one operating as the Internet developed, and remains the foundation of the international human rights system today.

4. DISCUSSION

4.1. EARLY HUMAN RIGHTS IMPLICATIONS OF THE INTERNET

By the 1990s, tensions were emerging between the openness and freedom of the Internet. Both were factors in its success, but also points of

41 Most recently in the UN Vienna Declaration of Human Rights (1993).

contention in debates about the Internet: a space where governments did not rule and where there were 'no good examples of how to govern such a rapidly changing and expanding resource in a consensual, integrative manner'.[42] On the one hand, like anyone else, governments were free to use the Internet for whatever they wanted; on the other hand, they could not control the freedom of other users, including their citizens, or those of other nations. Many countries operated state-owned telecommunications, many of which were monopolies charging exorbitant toll rates for national and international phone calls or faxes. Sending and receiving packets of data was quicker and cheaper than postal communications or the telephone, and journalists were among the first to seize the opportunities this presented. Initially, these were newspaper or radio journalists, recording their news stories in dangerous situations; they used the Internet to circumvent conventional telephone and mail surveillance by sending their stories via email (initially as simple text, but later including still images, and then videos).

Activists also established their own network infrastructure, through the likes of PeaceNet and GreenNet, who together established the first transatlantic computer link in 1987.[43] Environmental and peace activists were soon able to circumvent harassment, and interference with their postal communications, by using dial-up modems to connect to the Internet, allowing them to send and receive email in short bursts and then hang up. Other activist organisations, such as SANGONeT, were technical service providers, offering Internet connectivity, use of online bulletin board systems, technical training and website hosting to civil society organisations, trade unions and activists engaged in South Africa's anti-apartheid movement.[44] In some countries, such as those in the Middle East and North Africa, governments were largely unaware of the new technology, so democracy activists were able to share and upload content quickly and safely, and with a freedom not offered in state-run media or elsewhere.

---

42 J. HOFFMAN 'Critical Internet Resources: Coping with the Elephant in the Room'; in W. J. DRAKE (ed.), *Internet Governance: Creating Opportunities for All*, United Nations, New York 2010, pp. 1–14, at p. 1.

43 P. WILLETTS, 'Non-governmental Organisations in World Politics: The Construction of Global Governance' in T. G. WEISS and R. WILKINSON (eds.) *Routledge Global Institutions*, Routledge, Oxon 2011, pp. 95–100, at p. 96.

44 ibid., pp. 105–6 and 109. SANGONeT began as WorkNet, and is now NGO Pulse <https://www.ngopulse.org> accessed 22.06.2020.

In my initial research into this area, I found early adopters of the Internet reached for human rights as a way to articulate their freedom to create and use online spaces, and as a way to counter state or government interference with the Internet.[45] Perhaps the most famous example is John Perry Barlow's 'A Declaration of the Independence of Cyberspace', published online in February 1996. In response to proposed new laws to regulate the Internet, Barlow proclaimed with great rhetorical flourish:[46]

> Governments of the Industrial World, you weary giants of flesh and steel, I come from Cyberspace, the new home of Mind. On behalf of the future, I ask you of the past to leave us alone. You are not welcome among us. You have no sovereignty where we gather. We have no elected government, nor are we likely to have one, so I address you with no greater authority than that with which liberty itself always speaks. I declare the global social space we are building to be naturally independent of the tyrannies you seek to impose on us. You have no moral right to rule us nor do you possess any methods of enforcement we have true reason to fear.

Poetic defiance aside, Barlow's declaration captured well the underlying tensions between the Internet community and national governments. A new movement developed, advocating 'communication rights', a fourth generation of rights specific to the way the Internet worked, on the basis that the medium really did matter. Rather than focussing on freedom of the press, Daithí Mac Síthigh observed that communication rights emphasised the right to information, as well as related rights for citizens to have access to a diversity of news media, not only traditional media, which was often dominated by the interests of government monopolies or private corporations, or at the whim of media market forces.[47]

While they were concerned about the power of governments, civil society groups were also anxious that weak legal controls would enable corporations to act with impunity. They started with a simple application of existing human rights standards: after all, most governments had already agreed to these, as UN members. New charters and statements

---

45 J. LIDDICOAT, 'Human Rights Online: New Issues and Threats', 2011, Association for Progressive Communications <www.apc.org> accessed 11.05.2020.

46 J. P. BARLOW, 'A Declaration of the Independence of Cyberspace' Electronic Frontier Foundation, 08.02.1996 <https://www.eff.org/cyberspace-independence> accessed 11.05.2020.

47 D. MAC SÍTHIGH, 'From Freedom of Speech to the Right to Communicate' in M. E. PRICE, S. VERHULST and L. MORGAN (eds.), *Routledge Handbook of Media Law*, Routledge, London 2013, pp. 175–92.

of principles of human rights and the Internet emerged in regional bodies (such as the Council of Europe) and nationally (for example, in Estonia and Finland).[48] As will be explored further in Chapter 4, some multi-stakeholder groups developed new Internet rights charters; ways of expressing existing human rights in the context of the Internet.

But there was resistance to this engagement with human rights, especially from the private sector (which, as we saw earlier, considered human rights to be a matter for governments only), as well as the technical community (which did not want governments exerting control over how the Internet worked). As will be examined in Chapter 3, for example, the fundamental conceptual differences around accountability and the notion of 'who is in control' of the Internet (and even the very idea of control), as between the Internet and human rights communities, affected how long it took for the idea of human rights online to gain traction. For now, what is important to know is that the power struggle these tensions gave rise to was to pervade many aspects of the relationships between stakeholders, as well as their views about human rights and the Internet.

4.2. THE EMERGENCE OF INTERNET GOVERNANCE

Similar tensions also emerged in the UN, where different parts of the organisation were vying for leadership on various Internet-related matters. UNESCO, for example, developed position papers on rights to information, and to information communication technologies. Government members of the UN were becoming aware of the Internet, and competing with each other for some kind of role in its technical operation. Politics heavily infused discussion about the laws under which much of the Internet was coordinated, namely those of the United States of America, with debate arising about whether the domain name service (the system for dealing with IP addresses using names) should be managed in some other way.[49] The International Telecommunication Union (ITU), founded in the

48 C. WOODARD 'Estonia, Where Being Wired is a Human Right', *Christian Science Monitor*, 01.07.2003. In relation to Finland, the regulation was limited to technical connectivity standards for Internet access: see Ministry of Transport and Communications, 'Decree 732/2009 on the Minimum Rate of a Functional Internet Access as a Universal Service' (2009) (original: Liikenne- ja viestintäministeriön asetus tarkoituksenmukaisen Internet-yhtyeden vähimmäisnopeudesta yleispalvelussa <http://www.finlex.fi/en/laki/kaannokset/2009/en20090732> accessed 03.03.2021).

49 D. MAC SÍTHIGH, above n. 47, pp. 184–88.

late nineteenth century to coordinate global telegraph and telephone communication standards, was vying for a role in operating the new global Domain Name System.

This move was fiercely resisted by the technical community, which viewed the ITU with deep suspicion, and saw the government-led UN as highly political and, frankly, not relevant to the Internet, which was operating fine without them. The result was that Internet organisations, such as ICANN, were determined to eschew human rights as irrelevant to their mandate. I experienced this kind of response first hand at ICANN meetings I attended, and can well recall, for example, asking a question in a Governmental Advisory Committee meeting about human rights, only to have a very irate member of the business constituency lambast me afterwards, telling me that 'you cannot talk about human rights at ICANN'.

These clashes were understandable. While there are some similarities between the principles and processes of Internet standards-making and international human rights standards-making bodies (such as clear missions, aspirational goals and standards-based operations), there are also clear, fundamental, differences. The nature of the communities that participate in standards-making, their various roles, the ways in which standards evolve or apply to new developments, and their oversight and monitoring systems: all are quite different.[50]

In 2003, partly in response to these tensions, the United Nations convened a World Summit on the Information Society, known as the WSIS. The first Summit was unable to reach agreement on Internet governance and a working group was established to prepare recommendations for progress. At the second Summit in 2005 the pressure to have a forum focussing specifically on Internet policy and regulatory issues, led the WSIS to agree to establish an Internet Governance Forum (IGF) as a multi-stakeholder – rather than purely intergovernmental – forum to discuss the Internet.[51] This idea of 'governance' rather than 'government' emerged as an attempt to articulate and recognise the respective equal roles of many different groups (those multiple stakeholders, or 'multi-stakeholders' discussed earlier) who make the standards and protocols that help the Internet to operate. Internet governance was here: a new concept created, in part, by the increasing convergence of the Internet and human rights.

50 J. LIDDICOAT and A. DORIA, above n. 24, p. 5.

51 World Summit on the Information Society, United Nations and International Telecommunication Union (2005), WSIS Outcome Documents <http://www.itu.int/net/wsis/> accessed 03.03.2021.

Statements about international human rights were central to the WSIS, the related Geneva Declaration of Principles[52] and the IGF. This was important and significant progress, but despite these statements, meaningful discussion about the Internet in the international human rights system was virtually non-existent. By the end of 2010, for example, just a handful of references to the Internet had been made by the three UN human rights bodies.

Perhaps most tellingly, the supreme human rights body in the UN, the HRC, had never formally discussed the Internet. There was no clear guidance on how human rights were relevant online, no governments were reporting about Internet-related human rights issues, and only a very small handful of civil society groups were raising concerns in the HRC.[53] The gap between the Internet and the international system designed to protect human rights was wide, and showing no signs of closing.

52 Article 19 of the UDHR is cited in para. 4 of the Geneva Declaration of Principles (2003).

53 The Korean Progressive Network Jinbonet, founded in 1998, was one of the earliest Internet rights groups to engage with the Human Rights Council.

CHAPTER 2
THE EMERGENCE OF HUMAN RIGHTS ONLINE

1. INTRODUCTION

By early 2011, the Internet was in the midst of massive growth. New technologies were rapidly developing, as open Internet standards and protocols proliferated, and access increased from millions to billions of people. Like many others, activists reached for new Internet-based technologies to find each other, organise, and use the new tools in their work. They quickly saw the potential to use the Internet for highlighting human rights abuses, and creating and sharing news stories that mainstream media would not publish. The daily increase in Internet connectivity, and the creation and uploading of online content, saw offline struggles for human rights increasingly taken into online spaces, raising fundamental questions about whether human rights were relevant to the Internet and, if so, how. Many of the ways in which activists were using the Internet, and government responses to these, were challenging fundamental ideas about human rights.

2. THE PROMISE OF THE INTERNET

The Internet was often described as a kind of 'wild, wild West': a place where there were no laws and everyone was free to do as they pleased. But I have never liked that phrase. It connotes some kind of uncontrolled colonial expansion, evoking inglorious histories of unprincipled exploitation of people and land, or the claiming of property, simply because someone considered they were 'there for the taking', without recognising the multiple rights and interests of others. It evokes images of a 'gold rush' mentality.

I prefer to liken the expansion of the Internet to the early stages of the universe's evolution: the 'Big Bang': a time of formation, of creation of new and rapidly expanding stars and galaxies, spectacular dark holes, wondrous universes, and planets where all kinds of life began to flourish in different ecosystems. The Big Bang, in this case, was the emergence of the formative infrastructure needed to support Internet roll-out at different layers of the protocol stack, such as the rapid movement from telephone dial-up, and then to broadband connectivity and agreements to lay new undersea cables to connect continents.[1]

Those early days of Internet expansion were thrilling: here was a new way to connect with almost anyone in the world. Soon, the speed of Internet growth was breathtaking: between 2000 and 2015, the number of people using the Internet grew from 400 million to 3.2 billion – almost half the world's population.[2] It is hard to believe now, when the Internet is ubiquitous, and a generation of people has grown up knowing only global connectivity but, in 2011, websites were still considered 'billboards on the information highway' and the concept of a 'mobile Internet' was still new.[3] In the midst of this rapid growth were new opportunities and risks. By the end of 2010, the Internet, for many people, was still a place used largely for sending out information in one direction. The idea of user-generated content and online platforms was growing, but interactive online platforms were still relatively new, and social media had not yet globally emerged. This was the Internet that human rights activists were also beginning to explore, to try and understand how this new technology might be relevant to them, and help their work.

3. CASE STUDIES

The Internet offered new ways to empower citizens and participate in democratic movements. Citizen journalists began to use information communication technologies (ICTs) for daily tasks such as email, documenting evidence of human rights violations, and to assist with

---

1 By 2014, there were 285 communication cables on ocean floors: D. BROWN, 'Ten Facts about the Internet's Undersea Cables', *Mental Floss*, 12 November 2015 <https://www.mentalfloss.com/article/60150/10-facts-about-internets-undersea-cables> accessed 03.03.2021.

2 International Telecommunication Union, 'ICT Facts and Figures 2015', Geneva 2015 <https://www.itu.int/en/ITU-D/Statistics/Documents/facts/ICTFactsFigures2015.pdf> accessed 03.03.2021.

3 L. HORNER, 'A Human Rights Approach to the Mobile Internet' (Issue Paper, May 2011), Association for Progressive Communications <www.apc.org> accessed 03.03.2021.

advocacy, but this work also had its challenges.[4] Activists in different parts of the world were raising concerns about new types of interference with their activities.

3.1. EMAIL SURVEILLANCE

In early 2011, I was attending a digital security training course for human rights defenders, where Eunice (not her real name) recounted her recent experience of police harassment. She had been working in Ghana with a group of women advocating for prostitution law reform. Prostitution is illegal in Ghana, but sex work is widespread, with many women and girls vulnerable to exploitation.[5] Women's rights defenders were calling for law reform, better legal protection, a reduction in police harassment, and improved sexual and reproductive health and safety. Eunice advised us that the government was opposed to law reform, and there were reports of police harassment of activists.

Eunice and her friends were worried: their mail was being intercepted, with letters and parcels arriving to their offices already opened, and with obvious signs of having been interfered with. Sometimes the mail was not getting through at all. Worried about their telephones being bugged, and possible informants, they decided to plan one of their meetings via email, refraining from using phones or sending letters. They sent messages to each other via email only, and arranged to meet in the conference room of a hotel, under an innocuous-sounding booking reference.

On the appointed day, the women were optimistic that their plan had worked as, one by one, they arrived safely. Just as they sat down to start, there was a loud knock on the door. The women looked at each other wondering who it could be, as all of those expected were present and accounted for. Eunice answered the door and found herself confronted by two police officers who burst into the room. The officers demanded the women's identity documents, and told them they had to leave because their meeting was illegal. The women protested that they had done nothing wrong, to which the police responded: 'We know why you are meeting.

---

4 A. COMNINOS, 'Twitter Revolutions and Cyber-crackdowns: The Use of User-generated Content and Social Networking in the Arab Spring and Beyond' (Issue Paper, June 2011), Association for Progressive Communications <www.apc.org> accessed 03.03.2021.

5 United Nations, 'Combined Third, Fourth and Fifth Periodic Reports of States Parties: Ghana', Committee for the Elimination of All Forms of Discrimination Against Women, CEDAW/C/GHA/3-5, 18.04.2005, paras. 52–55, pp. 23–25.

You're talking about things that are illegal – sex, prostitution.' Threatening to arrest them, the police demanded that they disband their meeting and not return. Eunice and her friends decided to leave to avoid any more harassment, but were determined to work out how the police had found out about their meeting.

The women decided to check whether an email might have been sent to the wrong person, and asked a local Internet technician to look at their computers. The technician told them that their emails were insecure, and easily accessible by anyone who had access to the settings for the Internet service provider they were using. Eunice realised, with horror, that the police had been reading all of the emails they were sending to each other. The police had been able to access these easily, because the settings for the servers the emails were travelling on were insecure: there were no passwords protecting them, and the messages were not encrypted. This was the digital equivalent of sending a postcard through the mail, which anyone could read.

Eunice and her friends were outraged. Their privacy, their freedom of association, and their freedom of expression were under threat. Convinced that the police were deliberately harassing them, they feared for themselves and their family members, wondering whether they could take action against the police and, if not, how they could protect themselves. They were also upset that they had not been given basic training in how to secure their email traffic to make sure data packets could not be seen, by using passwords or encryption, for example. This is how Eunice came to attend our training.

Eunice was not alone in her concerns. Human rights defenders around the world were also noticing other disturbing trends. Just as the promise of the Internet as a powerful tool for promoting and protecting human rights was becoming apparent, there were worrying signs of governments acting to prevent people from accessing online content. Two broad themes emerged: new forms of well-known interferences with human rights, and new, Internet-specific ones.

3.2. SIGNAL JAMMING

Jamming radio broadcasts is a tactic to stop citizens receiving information from foreign countries. In World War II, the German government attempted to block broadcasts by the BBC to the European continent, and to counteract such broadcasts with their own airdrops of propaganda leaflets in London. The Soviet Union began jamming radio broadcasts in 1948, with targets including the Voice of America and Radio Liberty, and only finally ceased doing so in 1987.[6] Many other countries have jammed radio or satellite transmissions, including China, Francoist Spain, Iran, and both North and South Korea, with some alleging that the practice continued in countries such as Vietnam[7] and Ethiopia well into the twenty-first century.[8]

Now, activists reported, some governments were signal jamming, or blocking their access to parts of the Internet, in a variety of ways. In the first instance, access to the Internet relied upon deployment of network infrastructure: telecommunications infrastructure over which Internet traffic could travel. Reports were emerging that some governments were simply refusing, or unnecessarily delaying, the roll out of Internet infrastructure to certain politically sensitive areas, slowing down connection speeds, or centralising connection points to those with government control.[9] In other areas where Internet access was limited, citizens made use of local Internet cafes. However, citizens in Tunisia reported that law enforcement authorities were asking Internet cafe operators to monitor customers, and to require presentation of national identity cards before they could use a computer.[10]

Blocking access to online information (content blocking) was a new way to interfere with Internet access and use. Governments appeared to be embracing such new ways to control access to information, and there were some worrying examples. Pakistan, for instance, sought to ban the use of encryption software (including for email), with severe security and privacy implications for human rights activists like Eunice as well as journalists.[11]

---

6 J. P. McGREGOR 'Jamming of Western Radio Stations to the Soviet Union and Eastern Europe', Office of Research, United States Information Agency (April 1983), available at: <http://www.radiojamming.puslapiai.lt/doc_en.htm> accessed 11.04.2020.

7 BBG Watch, 'Radio Listeners, Vietnamese Shortwave Jammers Surprised and Confused by US Agency Cuts' (Commentary) (2014) <https://bbgwatch.com/bbgwatch/radio-listeners-vietnamese-shortwave-jammers-surprised-and-confused-by-u-s-agency-cuts/> accessed 11.04.2020.

8 BBC, 'Ethiopia Admits Jamming VOA Radio Broadcasts in Amharic' BBC News 19.03.2010 <https://news.bbc.co.uk/2/hi/8575749.stm> accessed 03.03.2021.

9 S. KELLY and S. COOK (eds.), *Freedom on the Net: A Global Assessment of Internet and Digital Media* Freedom House, Washington 2011, pp. 6–7.

10 A. COMNINOS, above n. 4, p. 7.

11 B. BUKOVSKA, 'Pakistan: Ban on Encryption a Violation of Freedom of Expression' (2011) Article 19, available at <https://www.refworld.org/docid/4e6608ce2.html> accessed 29.06.2020.

The indiscriminate and destabilising effect of such a ban would be widely felt, since encryption was used to provide secure banking and e-commerce, as well as to bypass the Pakistani government's regular blocking of entire websites.

3.3. ENTRAPMENT AND INFORMANTS

The use of spy informants with fake identities to infiltrate activist groups is an old entrapment tactic, and one very familiar to human rights defenders. But activists reported that new types of online spies and informants were appearing, such as 'sock puppets'. Sock puppets were fake online identities through which a person would operate much like a ventriloquist's dummy, impersonating a genuine supporter in order to infiltrate a group. After becoming involved in a Web-based forum or group, the sock puppet would use the fake identity to spy on and harass individual members. With the online nature of such forums and groups, members might easily be misled, or simply be unaware they were being spied upon, putting them at risk of disclosing their locations, being harassed about their views, or even being arrested and detained.[12]

In some cases, rather than create an individual fake identity, 'astroturfing' might be used to create artificial 'turf' for surveillance: entirely fake 'grass-roots' organisations. The aim, in these cases, was to make the fake organisation appear so authentic that people would be tricked into joining. Once signed up, their personal information (including political views) could be ascertained, documented, and then either passed to authorities, used to intimidate and harass them or their families offline, or simply used to spread misinformation about real organisations so as to discredit them.

3.4. INFORMATION FILTERING AND CONTENT BLOCKING

Content filtering is the practice of preventing access to certain types of information (text or images). It occurred in many ways, and human rights defenders were struggling to keep up with all of them. In the first instance, an organisation's website IP address might be identified, and domain name

---

[12] A. COMNINOS, above n. 4, p. 14.

service requests for it prevented from connecting. Alternatively, a specific domain name and related IP address could be identified and tampered with (such as pointing traffic to a non-existent or fake website such as www.intersentia.net instead of www.intersentia.com). In other cases, a specific URL might be blocked so that a particular web page rather than a whole website could not be found.[13]

Others noticed that search results had simply been removed from browser searches. This involved third parties, namely Internet search engine companies cooperating with governments or law enforcement agencies to block or remove a predetermined list of websites from appearing in web search results. This tactic did not result in the content being taken down or blocked, but simply made it much more difficult to find. A particularly insidious aspect of this tactic was that an innocent organisation might not realise that this was happening for quite some time, depending on how site traffic was monitored.[14]

New limitations on access to certain types of content were also on the increase. The use of laws against heresy or blasphemy to stifle political speech, for example, was not new, but human rights defenders were concerned about the emergence of so-called 'faith-based filtering': filtering out, or blocking access to, online political and other content based on its allegedly blasphemous nature.[15] In 2010, for example, the Pakistan Telecommunication Authority ordered Internet service providers to block Facebook, YouTube, Flickr and other websites, in response to a proposed online contest that proposed a day for drawing images of the Prophet Muhammad.[16] The Islamic Lawyers Association won an injunction against Facebook for 'objectionable' content; an injunction lifted once the page in question was removed. The incident followed one, in 2008, when the government of Pakistan inadvertently blocked access to YouTube for the entire world when it encountered a 'technical glitch' while trying to block domestic access to its IP address: unable to locate a specific one, the

---

13 For a useful overview see J. ZITTRAIN and R. PALFREY 'Reluctant Gatekeepers: Corporate Ethics on a Filtered Internet', in R. DEIBERT et al (eds.) *Access Denied: The Practice and Policy of Global Filtering*, MIT Press, Cambridge, MA 2008, pp. 108–9.

14 ibid.

15 H. NOMAN 'In the Name of God: Faith-based Filtering in Majority Muslim Countries' (Report) (2011), OpenNet Initiative <https://opennet.net/sites/opennet.net/files/ONI_NameofGod_1_08_2011.pdf> accessed 03.03.2021.

16 A. NARAYANAN, 'Citing Sacrilegious Content, Pakistan Bans YouTube', *Huffington Post* (21.05.2010), available at <https://www.huffpost.com/entry/after-banning-facebook-pa_n_584137> accessed 03.03.2021.

government performed an Internet Protocol block, inadvertently taking YouTube offline globally for two hours.[17]

Elsewhere, law enforcement agencies were blocking online content under laws relating to offline speech. In Thailand, for example, videos containing negative views about the king were blocked under *lèse-majesté* provisions of the Thai Criminal Code, which made it illegal to defame, insult or threaten the Thai royal family.[18]

In the offline world, censorship of the media, including radio, television and print news, was certainly not a new phenomenon. Now, however, the nature and extent of Internet censorship through content filtering was emerging as a new and very pressing concern. One of the more widely known examples was the so-called 'Great Firewall of China', a national filtering system on key aspects of Internet infrastructure that was created by the People's Republic of China, preventing domestic access to websites containing words such as 'democracy' and 'human rights'.[19] In other places, website blocking and content filtering were happening without clear lawful authority; lists of sites to be filtered were kept secret, and it was extremely hard to know which content was prohibited. It was also difficult to ascertain on what basis, and through which channels, legal reviews or challenges of decisions could be sought.[20]

3.5. CRIMINALISING ONLINE BEHAVIOUR

As well as old tactics taking on new forms, entirely new, Internet-specific forms of interference were starting to appear. In some countries, new Internet-related offences were introduced, sometimes with penalties more severe than for equivalent offline offences. In Azerbaijan, for example, the government criminalised online dissemination of 'misinformation'; soon

---

17 OpenNet Initiative 'Filtering: Country Profile – Pakistan' pp. 342–43, available at: <https://opennet.net/research/profiles/pakistan> accessed 03.03.2021.

18 A. SURLYAWONGKOL,'Walls of Fame, Witch Hunts and the Power of the Crowd' (Thai Netizen Network) in *Global Information Society Watch*, Association for Progressive Communications and Hivos 2011, pp. 245–48 <https://www.giswatch.org/en/2011> accessed 03.03.2021.

19 S. KELLY and S. COOK, above n. 9, pp. 4–5; and, for an excellent overview, see also R. MacKINNON, *Consent of the Networked: The Worldwide Struggle for Internet Freedom*, Basic Books, New York 2012.

20 J. ZITTRAIN and R. PALFREY, above n. 13.

after Skype and Wikipedia were identified as potential national security threats.[21]

One particular concern was the severity of punishments for online defamation. In 2009, for example, Pritya Mulyasari was given a fine of 204 million rupiah (USD 22,000) by the Indonesian authorities for online circulation of allegedly defamatory remarks she made in an email to family and friends about her treatment at a private hospital where she was misdiagnosed with dengue fever when she actually had mumps. The hospital sued Mulyasari for defamation, and she was prosecuted for defamation under the Criminal Code. The hospital ultimately dropped its lawsuit, but she was found guilty under the Electronic Transactions and Information Code, which had penalties of up to six years imprisonment for electronic transmissions containing 'libellous content'. Mulyasari was fined, and sentenced to one year on probation, a sentence upheld on appeal.[22] Both the conviction and sentence were, however, subsequently overturned in 2012 on further appeal to the Indonesian Supreme Court.[23]

New, punitive, intellectual property laws were also developing, featuring Internet disconnection as a punishment. France and the United Kingdom both passed 'three strikes' laws providing for disconnection of users from the Internet for breaches of copyright or digital economy laws.[24] Internet activists were concerned that these new laws set dangerous precedents, extending intellectual property rights unreasonably, and imposing disproportionately severe penalties.

Another worrying trend was the increase in criminal prosecutions for online speech. In the offline word, such offences were generally limited to

---

21 V. GOJAYEV, 'The Struggle for Internet Freedom in Azerbaijan' in *Global Information Society Watch 2011 Update 1*, pp. 25–33, at p. 29.

22 M. LIM, '@crossroads: Democratization and Corporatization of Media in Indonesia' (2010) Arizona State University and Ford Foundation, 22 <https://merlyna.files.wordpress.com/2019/02/lim_at_crossroads_2011.pdf> accessed 03.03.2020; F. THAJIB, 'Monitoring and Defending Freedom of Expression and Association on the Internet in Indonesia' in *Global Information Society Watch Update 1*, 2012, pp. 34–42.

23 A. SAHBANI and M. ARKYASA, 'Supreme Court Declared Pritya Mulyasari Not Guilty as Charged' Hukumonline, 19.09.2012.

24 Haute Autorité pour la Diffusion des Oeuvres et la Protection des Droits d'auteur sur Internet 2009 (France), and Digital Economy Act 2010, s. 10 (United Kingdom). The French law was later ruled unconstitutional: see R. WRAY, 'French anti-file-sharing law overturned' *The Guardian*, 10.06.2009 <https://www.theguardian.com/technology/2009/jun/10/france-hadopi-law-filesharing> accessed 11.04.2020.

crimes related to libel, defamation, violence (such as threats to kill) or very serious crimes such as terrorism. But human rights defenders reported the increasing use of defamation laws to harass and imprison journalists or citizen bloggers who were using the Internet. By the end of 2010, for example, more than 100 people in Vietnam, Iran and China were in jail for offences relating to blogging.[25]

These tensions between citizens' rights and governmental authority were about to go beyond the national level and receive global attention, as mass protests against the Mubarak regime in Egypt drew the eyes of the world to the streets of Cairo.

3.6. INTERNET SHUTDOWNS

I first met Alaa Abd El-Fattah, an Egyptian blogger, at the home of a friend in Johannesburg. It was 2011, and I joined Internet rights activists from Uganda, South Africa, Zimbabwe, Ecuador, Malaysia, England, Australia and Egypt as we caught up and shared stories over a simple shared meal. The relaxed atmosphere belied how extraordinarily difficult 2011 had been for many of those present. Alaa was a quiet, soft-spoken man with a warm, open face and a ready smile. But he had deep concerns for his country, and had been working for many years to bring to public attention the state of affairs there. He was taking some brief respite, and some of those present were very worried about what would happen to him on his return, as he was a well-known blogger who had previously been arrested by the Egyptian authorities.[26]

In 2011, the word 'blog' was still relatively new to the modern lexicon. An abbreviation of 'weblog' (which refers to a web log, or content logged on a website), the blog developed rapidly in the early part of the twenty-first century as a new way for citizen journalists to create and self-publish their content. No longer needing editorial access to mainstream media, and free from the physical demands of creating and distributing print media, the blog could be created, uploaded and hosted anywhere on the Internet

---

25 F. LA RUE 'Report of the Special Rapporteur on the Promotion and Protection of the Right to Freedom of Opinion and Expression' United Nations Human Rights Council 26.04.2011 (A/HRC/17/27) para. 35, p. 10.

26 E. ZUCKERMAN, 'Egyptian Blogger Detained for Participating in Peaceful Protest', 08.05.2006, available at <http://www.ethanzuckerman.com/blog/2006/05/08/egyptian-blogger-detained-for-participating-in-peaceful-protest/> accessed 12.04.2020.

within minutes.[27] The sheer volume of blog content soon resulted in a 'blogosphere', which grew rapidly as a space where bloggers from around the world could create media channels outside the corporate, mainstream or government-controlled media, sharing freely what was happening in their countries, and protecting their stories from censorship.[28]

Alaa was very prominent in the Egyptian blogosphere. A software developer and political activist, he had developed Arabic language versions of software and, together with Manal Bahey Al-Din Hassan, founded the Egyptian blog aggregators Manaala, and Omraneya, the former an award-winning blog aggregation platform used throughout the Middle East.[29] Egyptian bloggers had been able to use the Internet since early 2004, and it was one of the few unregulated spaces in which they could communicate with each other. State-owned and operated television stations, national media outlets, and print and radio media were all closely monitored by State authorities. In contrast, online spaces were less closely policed, and by early 2011 there were more than half a million bloggers in Egypt alone.[30] Egyptian citizens were using the Internet to create and pass information to each other, publishing online to highlight issues such as political and judicial corruption, torture of detainees by police, and violence against women, among many other concerns.[31] The political situation was deteriorating, and there were calls for President Mubarak to stand down. There was a particular focus on concerns about police brutality, with those campaigning for change issuing a call to congregate in Cairo's Tahrir Square on 25 January, National Police Day.

In the preceding days, from 14 January onwards, people had been sharing invitations to come to Tahrir Square to demonstrate peacefully against corruption, torture and unemployment. Numerous videos of police brutality circulated online, along with information about the planned demonstrations, such as legal information about peaceful assembly and

---

27 M. KEREN, *Blogosphere: The New Political Arena*, Lexington Books, Lanham, MD 2006.

28 R. ABDULLA, 'The Revolution *will* be Tweeted' *The Cairo Review of Global Affairs*, 3 (2011), 41–9, at 42–3, available at <https://www.thecairoreview.com/essays/the-revolution-will-be-tweeted/> accessed 15.04.2020.

29 Human Rights Watch, 'False Freedom: Online Freedom in the Middle East and North Africa' (Issue Paper) (2005) Vol. 17, No. 10, pp. 17–42 at p. 25.

30 R ABDULLA, above n. 28.

31 R. RAOOF, 'The Internet and Social Movements in North Africa' in *Global Information Society Watch*, Hivos and Association for Progressive Communications, 2011, pp. 38–41.

how to use online platforms and mobile phones to organise peacefully. A media tent was set up in the Square where bloggers, political activists and human rights defenders put up a sign which read 'place to upload pictures and videos', so that demonstrators could quickly share information.[32]

But, by 25 January, by which time thousands were gathering in Tahrir Square, the government was already cracking down on modes of communication, including the Internet and online platforms. Early that day, human rights defenders' mobile phones were shut down, and some platforms such as Twitter and Bambuser (a live video sharing platform) were blocked. The 3G network coverage in Tahrir Square was shut down completely and, the following day, Blackberry phone services were also shut down. That same day, the Internet across Egypt was shut down completely, except for one Internet service provider. At 10 p.m. on 27 January, SMS messaging was also shut down. Various newspaper websites were blocked, and landlines were disabled in some parts of Cairo. On 28 January, the government shut down mobile phone services for a day and, on 29 January, the news media outlet Al Jazeera Cairo was also shut down. Finally, on 31 January, the only Internet service provider still operating went dark.[33]

In the space of just six days, Egyptians and the wider world watched as, one by one, the lights went out on the Egyptian network; the first national Internet shutdown. It was not until 12.30 p.m. on 2 February that Internet services were restored. There was widespread public outrage at the Internet shutdowns, with a key concern being their indiscriminate impact. Many people reported not being able to use the Internet to share information about safe routes around the Square, to find family members, to determine safe routes to or from schools and hospitals, or to know when it was safe to go to the markets for food. Some viewed the shutdown as a political move, to both punish the protestors, and turn public attitude against them by negatively affecting the public at large.

Internet shutdowns by governments were not new.[34] In 2005, for example, the government of Nepal cut all international Internet connectivity after a declaration of martial law and, in 2007, Internet access was shut down in parts of Myanmar by the military junta. But shutdowns

---

32 ibid.

33 ibid.

34 P. HOWARD, S. AGARWAL, D. SHEETAL and M. HUSSAIN, 'When Do States Disconnect Their Digital Networks? Regime Responses to the Political Uses of Social Media' (2011) *The Communication Review*, 14:3, 216.

on the scale seen in Egypt were unprecedented and, a week afterwards, Mubarak resigned.

In the aftermath of the shutdowns, Egyptian activists demanded answers. There was fury at the actions of telecommunications companies, but also confusion, and debate about whether shutting down the Internet or interfering with network coverage were human rights violations. If they were, should companies that complied with government orders to shut down or interfere with the Internet and SMS communications be liable for any harms that resulted from their actions, for example to injured people who could not get to hospital because they could not call ambulances? Lawyers searched for grounds to file lawsuits. But telecommunications companies such as Vodafone defended their actions on the basis that the government directives in question had been made lawfully under Egyptian legislation. If the government actions were 'according to law', it was argued, there was nothing that those companies could do: were they to ignore the request, their managers faced potential imprisonment, and company licenses could be revoked.[35] In the end, the five-day Internet and telecommunications shutdown cost Egypt's economy at least USD 90 million.[36]

There was general agreement that the actions of the Egyptian government were unfair. Human Rights Watch, for example, issued a statement calling the shutdown 'an extreme step designed to disrupt planned marches, to block images of police brutality and to silence dissent once and for all', saying that 'the Egyptian government's unprecedented blackout of the nation's internet and most cell phone networks poses a major threat to basic human rights, and should be reversed immediately.'[37] But others struggled with the idea that Internet access should be treated in the same way as access to water, food or adequate housing.[38] Such people reasoned that the Internet had been back up and operating quickly, so there was no significant or long-lasting harm. At the same time, the government pushed

35 U. MULLER and S. PANDIT, 'Vodafone in Egypt: National Crises and their Implications for Multi-national Corporations' (Case Study) (2014) ESMT Berlin, available at <https://esmt.berlin/knowledge-article/vodafone-egypt> accessed 03.03.2021.

36 P. HOWARD et al, above n. 34, 231.

37 Human Rights Watch 'Nationwide Blackout Endangers Rights: Restore Web and Phone Networks for Egypt's Citizens', 28.01.2011 <https://www.hrw.org/news/2011/01/28/egypt-nationwide-internet-blackout-endangers-rights> accessed 03.03.2021.

38 D. SOUTER, 'Human Rights and the Internet: A Review of Perceptions' in *Human Rights Organisations*, Association for Progressive Communications, 2012, pp. 17–18 <https://www.apc.org/en/pubs/human-rights-and-internet-review-perceptions-human> accessed 03.03.2021.

back, saying that the crisis justified their actions as being necessary to protect national security. This confusion and debate added insult to injury for Egyptian activists.

Others, watching from abroad, coined the phrases 'Twitter revolution' and 'Democracy 2.0', convinced that the new ways of organising action heralded some kind of 'Arab Spring'. Egyptian activists considered such terms to be meaningless, misguided or ignorant. Ramy Raoof, for example, highlighted the role of social media, as 'online platforms were the media arm for Egyptians during the revolution, a space for Egyptians to share their experiences and thoughts and to show the truth of what had happened.'[39] Raoof noted that activists had been using the Internet and online digital platforms for years before the events in Tahrir Square, trying to highlight the gap between government-owned or national media outlets and the reality of daily life for citizens. The Internet and use of online platforms helped, but as Rasha Abdullah said, 'Facebook did not go to Tahrir Square. The people did. Twitter did not go to Al-Qaied Ibrahim Square. The people did.'[40]

Within a few months of returning to Egypt, Alaa Abd El-Fattah was arrested, destined to spend the next nine years in and out of prison.[41] Even today, as the Covid-19 pandemic spreads around the globe, Alaa is incarcerated and is on hunger strike demanding better prison conditions for his fellow inmates. Alaa's family and community continue to seek his release.[42] Egyptian activists and international supporters have not forgotten the power of the events in Tahrir Square, and the Internet shutdown which, at the time, brought into sharp relief the tensions between citizens' human rights, the authority of governments, and the battle for control of the Internet.

4. DISCUSSION

The case studies above highlight a diverse range of interferences with the Internet and online activities. These interferences were met with a variety

39 R. RAOOF, above n. 31.

40 R. ABDULLA, above n. 28.

41 J. SHENKER, 'Egyptian Revolutionary Alaa Abd El-Fattah Arrested by Junta', *The Guardian*, 31.10.2011 <https://www.theguardian.com/world/2011/oct/31/egyptian-junta-arrests-revolutionary-fattah> accessed 03.03.2021.

42 'Alaa on Hunger Strike to Protest Coronavirus Conditions' FreeAlaa, May 2020 <https://freealaa.net/en/about> accessed 03.03.2021.

of responses. Activists searched for new kinds of avoidance techniques that were sometimes in violation of the terms and conditions of their online providers, such as the use of pseudonyms. In 2011, for example, students from University College London were protesting against student fee increases and cuts to spending on education. Many were using Facebook profiles to organise action, using pseudonyms to protect their identities, due to the risk of offline harassment.[43] On the eve of planned peaceful protests, openDemocracy blogger Guy Aitchison reported that, in one 12-hour period, over 50 protestors' Facebook profiles had been deleted. While acknowledging that fake names were a violation of Facebook's policies, protestors were suspicious about the timing (which coincided with a royal wedding and the May Day weekend) saying, 'it was a scandalous abuse of power by Facebook to arbitrarily destroy online communities built up over many months and years. These groups provide a vital means for activist groups to communicate with their supporters.'[44] Activists called on Facebook to help reinstate pages, to which Facebook officially responded that profiles were for individuals only, not groups or businesses, and therefore accounts had been 'disabled for violating these guidelines'.[45]

Pseudonyms are often promoted as a useful identity protection tool, to prevent online harassers, or 'trolls'. Activists felt strongly that requiring real names on their profile pages, in all cases, made their work unsafe, and was unfair, violating their rights to free speech and to freedom of association. But there were no clear complaint mechanisms for challenging Facebook's actions.[46] In addition, activists were suspicious that law enforcement agencies were following online profiles closely, and providing lists to Facebook of those that they wanted disabled. Combined with other practices such as the filtering and removal of user-generated content from social networks without notice, and with no apparent rights of review or

---

43 J. RUIZ, 'Cutting to the Core: The Role of Social Media in Resistance in the UK', in *Global Information Society Watch*, Association for Progressive Communications and Hivos, 2011, pp. 253–58.

44 G. AITCHISON, 'Political Purge of UK Facebook Underway', OurKingdom, 29.04.2011 <www.opendemocracy.net/ourkingdom/guy-aitchison/political-purge-of-uk-facebook-underway> accessed 29.06.2020.

45 Anticutsspace, 'Facebook Forced to Respond to our Campaign for Restoration of Accounts' 29.04.2011, available at <https://anticutsspace.wordpress.com/2011/04/29/facebook-forced-to-respond-to-our-campaign-for-restoration-of-accounts/> accessed 29.06.2020.

46 A. COMNINOS, above n. 4.

remediation, activists worried that they were powerless to legally challenge these actions.

Indeed, by 2011, some commentators had concluded that the balance of power between citizens and governments had already shifted, and that the promise of a free and open Internet was under significant threat. Some argued that the promise and power of online freedom was dissipating, and that new forms, and new norms, of information control techniques specific to the Internet had emerged.[47] Autocratic governments appeared to be embracing the new technologies, using these in new ways to infiltrate lawful groups, carry out surveillance, and illegally disrupt the activities of human rights defenders. Democratic governments, too, were not immune from these tactics, and there was evidence that they were no longer shying away from calling for regulation of the Internet, as they had in the era of communication rights.

Instead, many national governments were actively promoting their duties under the international human rights system, invoking their obligations as states to protect human rights as the reason for attempting to regulate the Internet. They cited such grounds as national security, prevention of child sexual exploitation, and prevention of other criminal activity. Tensions were emerging between the role of government in protecting public order, and citizens' rights to freedom of expression and freedom of association. In the wake of the London riots in 2011, for example, the British prime minister asserted that control of access to the Internet and social networking sites was a legitimate riot-control option for the British authorities.[48] Facebook was not alone in being criticised for the practices of account deactivation, and apparently arbitrary or unfair use of terms of service and community guidelines. Twitter, Flickr and Blogger were also criticised for account deactivations, and use of their terms of service to police online content.[49]

Attempts to understand these new interferences as human rights violations were complicated by the ways in which people were using the Internet, and whether they perceived the Internet differently, in human rights terms, from other kinds of technology. It seems odd now, but

---

[47] R. DEIBERT, J. PALFREY, R. ROHOZINSKI and J. ZITTRAIN (eds.), *Access Controlled: The Shaping of Power, Rights, and Rule in Cyberspace*, MIT Press, Cambridge, MA 2010.

[48] J. RUIZ, above n. 43, p. 258.

[49] J. YORK, 'Policing Content in the Quasi-Public Sphere' *OpenNet Initiative Bulletin*, September 2010 <https://opennet.net/policing-content-quasi-public-sphere> accessed 03.03.2021.

I remember my surprise and delight the first time I witnessed the power of a 'Twitterfall'. I was at a meeting in Stockholm about an upcoming report by Frank La Rue, who was the United Nations Special Rapporteur on the right to freedom of expression. His would be the first report to the UN Human Rights Council to focus on the Internet and human rights. Various eminent speakers were onstage, and members of the large audience were invited to participate by tweeting to the event hashtag.

The tweets displayed in real time on a screen behind the panellists, appearing to fall down the screen like the flow of a waterfall. Seeing speakers being fact-checked in real time – their statements immediately corrected or corroborated, applauded or rebuked – was magical. All of this happened as panellists were speaking; to my amazement, some of the panellists even tweeted themselves. The moderator took questions from the audience via the Twitter feed, instead of waiting for the usual few assertive people to ask questions. I remember wondering whether I was online or offline, or both at the same time.

Looking back, my naivety feels embarrassing. But that, in a nutshell, was the conceptual barrier for human rights advocates: online or offline. In the real, physical world, we were eating, sleeping, walking, driving, loving and playing. We did not *live* on the Internet any more than we lived inside the television or the telephone. The Internet was not a place like our home, a building, or a park. It was just a computer screen with a keyboard connected to other computers: a tool for writing, sending and viewing our words and images.

Conventional human rights thinking, at that time, was that the Internet might appear magical, but it was not, and could not be, a multi-dimensional space: so how could human rights apply *on* the Internet? To talk of 'Internet rights' or 'human rights online', so this line of thinking went, was to entirely miss the point that human rights belonged to people, not networked computers.[50]

My Twitterfall experience introduced me to a new way of thinking about the Internet as a space connected in real time to the physical world, each shaping the other. Of course human rights belonged to people and, yes, the Internet was not the same as our physical world. But humans have not always lived in cities, attended schools, or worked in factories and offices: we create new spaces with new rights. As I began to work with activists, I saw that to view the Internet as just a tool was to miss

---

50 ibid., pp. 32–34.

something significant. The Internet was not just a tool; it was becoming another dimension, another place where human rights defenders lived, that could be safer for them than their offline homes and offices. As one activist put it, the Internet was not a tool, like some new kind of spade to dig the garden: the Internet *was* the garden.[51]

51 J. KEE, conversation with author, 2011.

CHAPTER 3
HUMAN RIGHTS VIOLATIONS

1. THE CONCEPTUAL CHALLENGES

Despite the powerful events in the Middle East and North Africa during the early twenty-first century, the concept of human rights online struggled to gain credence. Few mainstream human rights organisations focussed on the Internet and, as a Human Rights Commissioner in New Zealand, I focussed on the more obvious 'offline' human rights issues: discrimination, harassment, violence against women, the rights of gender and sexual minorities, and democratic rights. Those of us working on offline human rights did not recognise that the Internet was a political space where human rights were relevant and under threat.

Our ignorance was understandable: after all, the government tactics complained of were hardly new. Surveillance, harassment, arrest, detention and torture: these have been the tactics of despots and tyrants for millennia. There were several other causes of our ignorance in the early 2010s. Many human rights organisations were deeply immersed in their existing work (whether children's rights, poverty, racism or the emerging issue of climate change), and felt unable to engage in 'new' issues like the Internet, even though the Internet had been developing for many years.[1] Few such organisations were using the Internet (other than, perhaps, for email and a rudimentary website), partly because funders would not provide additional money for computer equipment, and partly because they lacked the capacity and capability to develop and use Internet technologies. Few had social media accounts or used online platforms, which themselves were still in relatively early development.[2]

---

1 See, for example, P. WHALEY, 'Human Rights NGOs: Our Love-Hate Relationship with the Internet' in S. HICK, E. F. HALPIN and E. HOSKINS (eds.), *Human Rights and the Internet*, Macmillan Press, London 2000, pp. 30–40.

2 D. SOUTER, 'Human Rights and the Internet: A Review of Perceptions' in *Human Rights Organisations*, Association for Progressive Communications, 2012, pp. 30–34

In addition, there were simpler, conceptual challenges to overcome. Back then, I often felt bemused by discussions about human rights and the Internet – like a first year student at the wrong lecture. Then, many human rights advocates, myself included, were struggling to understand:

- how an Internet interference could be a human rights violation; and
- who ought to be accountable for Internet-related human rights violations.

We were in the space where understanding is only just beginning: that place between theory and practice; the messy reality of the emerging field of human rights online.

2. WHAT IS A HUMAN RIGHTS VIOLATION?

Injustice is a deep-seated cultural, social and political construct.[3] As infants, we can learn to associate feelings of fear or anger with injustice before we can talk or walk.[4] As we grow and mature, concepts of injustice expand from the very simple to the complex, helping us to shape, and make sense of, the world around us. It is one thing to feel anger and a sense of injustice over your postcard being read by someone to whom it was not addressed, being followed around in public spaces online, or by the enforcement of 'real name' policies by Facebook; but a feeling of anger or sense of injustice, however deep-seated and understandable, does not necessarily make for a human rights violation. This raises the question of where the concerns of Internet activists fit within a modern legal approach to human rights.[5]

A typical response to the question, 'what is a human rights violation?' might, for example be 'someone imprisoned unfairly'. A classic example of such a case is that of the two Portuguese students arrested, and sentenced to seven years in jail, for raising their glasses in a toast for freedom

<https://www.apc.org/en/pubs/human-rights-and-internet-review-perceptions-human> accessed 03.03.2021.

3 A. SEN, *The Idea of Justice*, Penguin Books, London 2009.

4 L. FELDMAN BARRETT, *How Emotions Are Made: The Secret Life of the Brain*, PanMacMillan, London 2018, pp. 99–104.

5 By 'modern legal approach', I mean the international human rights system outlined in Chapter 1.

in 1960. After learning of their plight, Englishman Peter Benenson issued a public call to unite in the protection of prisoners of conscience around the world, and Amnesty International was born.[6] Today, examples of human rights violations are well recognised: imprisonment without proper legal basis, unjust deprivation of liberty for political reasons, or discrimination or harassment simply for exercising rights to freedom of expression or peaceful protest.

While, for most, the concept of a human rights violation is typically a broad one, for lawyers it has a much more precise definition. Just as Internet service providers do not 'run the Internet', nor is every concern or perceived injustice a human rights violation that demands a remedy. We might be concerned about the high cost of technology, for example, but that does not mean that we all have a right to free computers. When, therefore, does an interference with our use of the Internet, however unjust it might appear, meet the legal definition of a human rights violation?

Despite its widespread everyday use, there is no single, generic definition of the term 'human rights violation'.[7] An extensive review of major human rights standards, human rights resources, handbooks, guidance documents, frequently asked questions, and even glossaries will not provide a clear answer to the simple question: what is the definition of a human rights violation? Instead, you will find a myriad of references to human rights violations of many kinds, each defined in their own specific contexts. In relation to the International Covenant on Civil and Political Rights (ICCPR), for example, guidance by the UN Human Rights Committee sets out the duties of states, including the obligation to provide reparations for individuals whose rights 'have been violated', and uses terminology such as 'States committing violations', without defining what a violation is.[8] Depending on the context, the legal definition can seem so complex to the average person that Ken Roth of Human Rights Watch once encouraged a simple focus on reporting injustice, rather than

6 P. BENENSON 'The Forgotten Prisoners', *The Observer*, 28.05.1961. An abridged archived version of the original article is available in The Guardian archives: <https://www.theguardian.com/uk/1961/may/28/fromthearchive.theguardian> accessed 03.03.2021.

7 See, e.g. the United Nations Human Rights Council publications and resources at <https://www.ohchr.org/EN/PublicationsResources/Pages/Publications.aspx> accessed 09.11.2020.

8 Human Rights Committee, 'General Comment 31 on the Nature of General Legal Obligations Imposed on States Parties to the Covenant' (29.03.2004), CCPR/C/21/Rev.1/Add. 13, paras. 16–20, pp. 6–8.

getting 'all caught up in the legalisms'.[9] Likewise, the UN Office of the High Commissioner for Human Rights (OHCHR) has observed that 'there is no single or official definition' of human rights impact assessments.[10]

For present purposes, namely a very simple introduction to the relevant concepts, we can safely say that a human rights violation generally has three elements:

(a) a legally recognised right with a correlating rights-holder and duty-bearer;
(b) an interference with that right, which results in harm; and
(c) a legal remedy for that harm.

Regarding the arrest of the freedom-toasting Portuguese students, for example, there was a right to be free from unlawful detention; both students were rights-holders and the Portuguese government was a duty-bearer, responsible for protecting and respecting the students' rights. There was an interference (arrest on spurious grounds) and harm (the resulting imprisonment and deprivation of liberty). There was a legal remedy for that harm: the right to seek judicial review for release from prison. The arrest and detention of the students was, therefore, a human rights violation.

This simple, three-pronged approach to defining a human rights violation accords with that generally taken in the UN, such as by the OHCHR and treaty bodies.[11] In practice, proving a human rights violation can be very difficult, as detailed criteria apply to the three elements, depending on each particular case and the rights and freedoms involved. Each right and freedom also has specific elements, such as freedom of expression, freedom of association and the right to privacy. The relevant laws, and the specific evidence needed to prove a breach thereof, can also vary greatly from country to country. This general approach will

---

9 K. ROTH, 'How do you Know if Something is a Human Rights Violation' Human Rights Watch, 29.05.2015, available at <https://www.hrw.org/students-and-educators> accessed 09.11.2020.

10 S.WALKER, 'Human Rights Impact Assessments: Emerging Practice and Challenges' in E. RIEDEL, G. GIACCA and C. GOLAY, *Economic, Social and Cultural Rights in International Law: Contemporary Issues and Challenges*, Oxford University Press, Oxford 2014, pp. 391–416, at p. 395.

11 See, for example, OHCHR 'Who's Responsible? Attributing Individual Responsibility for Violations of International Human Rights and Humanitarian Law' in *United Nations Commissions of Inquiry, Fact-finding Missions and other Investigations* (2018), HR/PUB/18/3; and Human Rights Committee, above n. 8.

help, however, to understand why there were conceptual problems with establishing interference with the Internet as a human rights violation. As we shall see, allegations of Internet 'human rights violations' of the kind discussed in Chapter 2 generated much debate about all three elements.

2.1. CASE STUDIES

2.1.1. Enforcement of 'Real Name' Policies

Take an example discussed earlier in this book: enforcement of Facebook's 'real name' policies. The first steps in assessing an Internet-related human rights violation were to determine which rights were relevant to the actions complained of, who could assert these rights (the rights-holders), and whether anyone was under a duty to respect or protect those rights (duty-bearers).

In relation to identifying the relevant rights, even a cursory look at international human rights standards revealed good reasons for conceptual problems: did these even apply to the Internet? There was no single definition of 'human rights', and no complete list of all such rights.[12] Most of the international standards, such as the ICCPR, did not refer to the Internet, or even electronic communication, since they predated the invention of the Internet, dating from a time when no one had envisaged global online platforms such as Twitter or Facebook.[13]

Instead, most such standards were technologically neutral, with no references to technology of any kind. This drafting style has its advantages, since it is designed to avoid arguments about how human rights law applies to every new invention. It is a handy approach; after all, people keep inventing all sorts of things: electricity, the telephone, cars, computers. It would be impossible to update laws all the time.[14] But this made things

12 For an overview, see, e.g. M. SEPULVEDA et al, *Human Rights Reference Handbook*, 3rd ed., University for Peace, Costa Rica 2004, p. 6.

13 Notable exceptions include The Convention on the Rights of the Child, and the Convention on the Rights of People with Disabilities, which were both negotiated during the Internet era.

14 Some specific references to Internet-related technology started to appear in human rights standards in the mid-2000s. For example, the Convention on the Rights of Disabled People refers to the obligation of states to ensure that disabled persons have access to new kinds of information communication technologies. However, the purpose of the reference was to promote disabled persons' access to technology as a tool or aid, not to define human rights violations online, or to clarify whether disabled peoples' human rights applied online.

difficult when discussing interferences with the Internet and their human rights implications, even if it was assumed that these standards did apply.

In this case, which rights were relevant? Individual rights to freedom of expression and freedom of association applied offline, but how did these apply to individual users of Facebook? There was no *right* to be a Facebook member: people who joined signed a private contract agreeing to the company's terms and conditions, including rules about online standards of behaviour, and the 'real name' policy for individual profiles. Private contractual rights like these kinds of terms and conditions were not subject to the international human rights treaty system.

If this view was wrong, and rights to freedom of expression or freedom of association were somehow relevant to such a private contractual arrangement, *how* were they relevant? Did the right to freedom of association and peaceful assembly somehow include the freedom to join an online group such as Facebook? Did the right to freedom of expression apply in a private online group, rather than one that was open to the public? Could these rights be restricted and, if so, was a 'real name' policy a reasonable and lawful limitation?

The second question related to the identity of the duty-bearer responsible for respecting and protecting the relevant right. As noted in Chapter 1, international human rights duty-bearers are governments, not the private sector, which has traditionally sat outside of the international human rights system. If Facebook was not a duty-bearer under international human rights law, then how could the request for enforcement of the 'real name' policy be a human rights violation? Private litigation might be possible, based on the terms and conditions in the contract, so the argument went, but not on the basis of a human rights violation.

If the government was a duty-bearer, what were its duties? For example, did the government have a duty not to interfere with online freedom of expression or freedom of online assembly? How did this duty relate to its other human rights obligations, such as the duty to satisfy itself that demonstrations were peaceful? Was it unlawful for government authorities to monitor a public online space that was open for anyone to view (much like a public square)? Was it lawful for law enforcement agencies to raise complaints if they observed that some users were not complying with Facebook's terms and conditions?

Even if the existence of rights, rights-holders and a duty-bearer could be determined, there could be confusion as to the specific action constituting the interference. Was Facebook not simply applying the rules that users had already agreed to – terms and conditions limiting their speech and behaviour – when they signed up as members? If so, where was the interference with their human rights? Law enforcement agencies were simply asking Facebook to apply its own rules against the protestors it had under surveillance. How could asking a company to enforce its own policies be illegal?

A further difficulty was the nature of the harm, which was more difficult to establish and quantify. After all, Facebook had advised users that they were free to create an additional group profile, rather than an individual one, and to continue with their activities. While changing Facebook profiles might be annoying, there was no physical harm, but rather disruption to the organisation of an event. Even if this was a 'harm,' how bad was it: could it even be quantified?

Finally, what kind of remedy would be appropriate? Activists sought reinstatement of personal Facebook accounts: a remedy that, while important to them, seemed difficult to frame in clear legal terms and, to mainstream human rights lawyers, seemed hardly commensurate with the typical remedies for human rights violations offline. Facebook's actions were clearly disruptive, but the harm did not seem to be financial, or similar to the kind of severe emotional distress caused, for example, by false imprisonment.

These conceptual difficulties caused significant debate, some of which continues today, on issues such as whether social media companies and private online platform providers are duty-bearers.[15] But, in 2011, these issues were new, and there was relatively little literature. Caught between slow-moving human rights law and a fast-moving Internet, the situation was very confusing. Clearer, more concrete connections to existing definitions of human rights were needed. Fortunately, one such connection was about to be made in Spain, where a man seeking to keep his past a secret was about to become world-famous.

2.1.2. The So-Called 'Right to be Forgotten'

In 2010, Costeja González lodged a complaint with the Spanish Data Protection Authority (AEPD) against the daily newspaper *La Vanguardia Ediciones SL*, Google Spain, and Google Inc. Mr González complained that, when he had searched for his name using the Google search

15 See, e.g. A. CALLAMARD, 'The Human Rights Obligations of Non-state Actors' in R. F. JORGENSEN (ed.), *Human Rights in the Age of Platforms*, MIT Press, Cambridge, MA 2019, pp. 191–225.

engine in 2009, two prominent results had appeared, both relating to home foreclosure notices against him, published in 1998 when he was, temporarily, in financial trouble. The notices were old, but *La Vanguardia* had recently digitised and posted its entire records online. Mr Gonzalez's search results now contained links to two pages of *La Vanguardia*, dating from 19 January and 9 March 1998, on which an announcement mentioning his name appeared in connection with a real estate auction to recover social security debts.[16]

Mr González's case was based on his right to privacy, and protection of his personal information: specifically, the right to access personal information held about him, and the right to have this information corrected if it is wrong. He sought two main remedies. The first remedy sought was that *La Vanguardia* either remove or alter the relevant web pages so that the personal data relating to him no longer appeared, or that it apply certain filtering tools made available by search engines, to protect the data from appearing on those pages. Second, he requested that Google Spain or Google Inc. remove or conceal the personal data relating to him, so that the notices were not included in Google search engine results, or in the links to *La Vanguardia*.

In 2010, the AEPD rejected the complaint against *La Vanguardia*, saying that publication was legally justified by order of the Ministry of Labour and Social Affairs: there had been no invasion of privacy. After all, part of the punishment for failing to pay debts is public notice to the community, and to other possible creditors. However, the AEPD accepted the complaint against Google Spain and Google Inc. They ruled that search engine operators were subject to data protection law because they carry out data processing for which they are responsible, and 'they act as intermediaries in the information society'.[17]

The AEPD decided that it had the power to direct Google to withdraw the data, and prohibit access to it, including at the request of a person who did not want others to see it, like Mr González. While the *La Vanguardia* website could lawfully host the content, the AEPD considered that Google could be required to remove it from their search engine results, so that this information about Mr González could be forgotten.

The case linked to existing human rights, and well-established principles of what the French called 'the right to oblivion', and those in the

---

16 Case C-13112, *Google Spain & Google Inc v Agencia Espanola de Proteccion de Datos and M C González*, European Court of Justice ECLI:EU:C:2014:317.

17 ibid., para. 17.

United States of America called 'practical obscurity'. These principles are based on the premise that privacy can grow back over time, since what is news today is gradually forgotten, and no longer in the public domain.[18] Founded on the same principles, the concept of a 'right to be forgotten' quickly caught on with Internet law commentators and policymakers, picking up momentum as Mr González's case progressed.

The decision was appealed to the European Court of Justice, where the Spanish, Polish, Italian and Austrian governments, as well as the European Commission, joined the case and made legal arguments. The Court upheld the AEPD decision, ruling that Google Inc. and Google Spain should break links to the old newspaper stories about Mr González's debt.[19] Google accepted the Court's decision, and responded by making available a form for European Union citizens to request the removal of links to material that they considered to breach their information privacy.

The case received unprecedented publicity and commentary, but the legal points were, in fact, very limited: the judgment did not establish a general right to be forgotten, and implementation by Google did not have the effect of the Internet 'forgetting' information about Mr González or anyone else. It simply required Google to remove or delist links returned in search results, based on an individual's name, when those results were 'inadequate, irrelevant or no longer relevant, or excessive'. Google was not required to remove or delist results in all cases, for example it was not required to remove them if there was an overriding public interest in the results, 'such as the role played by the data subject in public life'.[20]

The power of this case lay in its simple application of existing law to the Internet: in particular, to a company operating a search engine. The case proved that some national human rights laws, such as those protecting the right to privacy and personal information, could apply to the Internet. While the case was not without controversy, even among Internet activists,[21] it was useful for more mainstream human rights defenders, as it showed how an Internet interference could be a human rights violation.

---

18 For a useful overview, see J. ROSEN, 'The Right to be Forgotten' (2012) 64 *Stanford Law Review* 88.

19 ibid.

20 *González*, above n. 16, at para. 94 of the ruling.

21 See, e.g. concerns about misuse raised in Access Now, 'Understanding the Right to Be Forgotten' (Position Paper), September 2016 <https://www.accessnow.org/cms/assets/uploads/2017/09/RTBF_Sep_2016.pdf> accessed 03.03.2021.

2.1.3. *Discussion*

Looking back, the *González* case was not such a difficult conceptual leap. After all, other countries were linking the Internet to existing human rights. In India, for example, a campaign regarding the right to information culminated in the government passing a law establishing a right for citizens to request information from public agencies.[22] The Right to Information Act requires every public authority to provide information to the public at regular intervals 'through various means of communications, including the internet' so that the public have minimal need to invoke the Act to obtain information.[23] But the conceptual difficulties were very real at the time. By early 2011, while there was progress in some areas, this was largely iterative, occurring in response to specific litigation or campaigns. In general, human rights lawyers were still finding it difficult to understand interferences with the Internet within existing definitions of human rights violations.[24] Two other areas of conceptual difficulty were definitions of harm, and the identification of remedies, and these are discussed below.

2.2. DEFINITIONS OF HARM ONLINE

To be a 'human rights violation', there must be an interference with a right or freedom (which can be an act or an omission), and that interference must cause some kind of significant harm. For example, if you leave the door to your house open, but no one walks in, there has been no harm – no 'invasion' of your privacy. The harm must be caused by the actions you are complaining about, and be direct (such as deprivation caused by segregating people based on their race) or indirect (such as disabled people not being able to get to work because a transport provider inadvertently assumes that all people who use public transport are able-bodied).

---

22 O. MANZAR and R. SRIVASTAVA, 'The Role of the Internet in the Right to Information in India' in *Global Information Society Watch*, Association for Progressive Communications and Hivos, 2011, pp. 136–39, at pp. 136–37 <https://www.giswatch.org/en/2011> accessed 03.03.2021.

23 Right to Information Act 2005, s. 4(2) (India).

24 See, for example, M. L. BEST, 'Can the Internet be a Human Right?' *Human Rights and Human Welfare* 4 (2004) 23–31, 25 <https://www.du.edu/korbel/hrhw/volumes/2004/best-2004.pdf> accessed 03.03.2021.

The harm must be quantifiable, for example physical injuries sustained in an assault, emotional (shock or humiliation), reputational (loss of face in the eyes of the public) or financial (loss of income, or the incurrence of extra costs). In the case of Mr González, for instance, the harm was reputational.

A key conceptual challenge, linked closely to the online/offline distinction, was the question of whether there could be harm *on* the Internet. In the case of Mr González, the harm was clearly defined: ongoing reputational damage. But what about other kinds of harm? Could violence be perpetrated online? Could emotional or financial harm occur online? If so, was this 'real' harm, as traditionally defined? If there could be harm online, what was the remedy? Who was accountable for harms online?

Women's human rights defenders were at the forefront of this conceptual challenge: reporting both the new ways in which technology was being used to perpetrate violence against women offline, and new forms of violence against women online. Violence against women is a serious global concern: in 2012 an estimated 35 per cent of women experienced physical and/or sexual intimate partner violence, or non-partner sexual violence, and over a third of all murders of women were committed by an intimate partner.[25] There were reports that this violence was spreading online, with violence against women being 'committed, abetted or aggravated through the use of ICTs and in online spaces'.[26] In the same way that women faced 'offline' risks in the home or on the streets, violence was turning the Internet into an unsafe *online* space, with specific dangers and risks for women.

New forms of online violence against women included cyberstalking (following a woman's activity on the Internet), online harassment, image manipulation (such as circulating fake sexually explicit images to degrade or humiliate), privacy violations by individuals, or online mob-style attacks aimed at creating fear, causing real psychological harm and limiting participation in public life.

A prominent case was that of Khadija Ismayilova, Azerbaijan's leading investigative female journalist, well known for her radio show reporting

25 World Health Organization and others, *Global and Regional Estimates of Violence against Women: Prevalence and Health Effects of Intimate Partner Violence and Non-partner Sexual Violence*, Switzerland 2013.

26 J. MOOLMAN, 'The Need to Prioritise Violence against Women Online' in *Global Information Society Watch*, Association for Progressive Communications and Hivos, 2013, pp. 38–41, at p. 38 <https://www.giswatch.org/2013-womens-rights-gender-and-icts> accessed 03.03.2021.

political corruption.[27] In 2011, she was subjected to a blackmail attempt, after unknown sources secretly filmed her and her boyfriend at home. Ismayilova was threatened with blackmail and posting of the video online, unless she 'behaved'. Angry at the threat, she decided not to give in, continuing her show and reporting the attempt to authorities. Soon afterwards, the video was sent anonymously to a variety of media outlets, and posted to a website purporting to be that of the New Equality Party, a political opponent of the ruling New Azerbaijan Party.[28]

I had the privilege of meeting Khadija Ismayilova in 2012, and her steely courage was striking. I was working for the Association for Progressive Communications at the Internet Governance Forum in Baku. Before going, we agreed to try to support the Azerbaijani community, and I organised a dinner for local activists. It was an opportunity for journalists, academics, civil society groups and others to relax and network informally, learn of each other's concerns, and share support.

Khadija was impressive: a woman standing up to one of the most corrupt countries in Europe, chatting amiably over dinner with other journalists, one of whom had been imprisoned by authorities under apartheid South Africa. Following the release of the video, Khadija had feared for her life in religiously conservative Azerbaijan, where 'honour killings' still took place. She had worried that it would spark physical attacks, in addition to the death threats that she was already receiving. In a move that Khadija later said 'could have saved my life', conservative religious leaders strongly denounced the blackmail, demanding that it stop.[29] When we met in 2012, the International Women's Media Foundation had just awarded her the Courage in Journalism Award,[30] but safety concerns remained. This was real harm – blackmail and threats – linked to both online and offline spaces.

Another prominent case involved Anita Sarkeesian, a Canadian-American pop culture media critic, and founder of Feminist Frequency, a website hosting content analysing portrayals of women in popular culture.

---

27 V. GOJAYEV, 'The Struggle for Internet Freedom in Azerbaijan' in *Global Information Society Watch, Special Edition* Association for Progressive Communications and Hivos, 2011, pp. 25–33, p. 32 <https://www.giswatch.org/en/2011> accessed 03.03.2021.

28 B. BRUMFIELD, 'Salacious Video Defames Journalist Critical of Azerbaijani Government', CNN, 20.03.2012, available at <https://edition.cnn.com/2012/03/19/world/asia/azerbaijan-video-defamation/index.html> accessed 23.06.2020.

29 ibid.

30 International Women's Media Foundation, 'Khadija Ismayilova: 2012 Courage in Journalism Award'. Available at <https://www.iwmf.org/2012/10/khadija-ismayilova-2012-courage-in-journalism-award/> accessed 29.04.2020.

In 2011, Sarkeesian started a Kickstarter page seeking crowdsourced funding of $6,000 for a study on 'Tropes V Women in Video Games', a series of videos exploring tropes (figurative language or depictions) of female character stereotypes in gaming industry history.[31] The project prompted an unprecedented campaign against her, including death threats, calls for her to be gang-raped, and emails containing images of her being raped by video game characters. One person created a video game, called *Beat up Anita Sarkeesian*, that prompted players to 'beat up' depictions of Sarkeesian until 'blood' appeared on the game screen.[32] But the online backlash also created a surge of support: her treatment caused outrage, amplifying concerns for women in the gaming industry, leading to almost $160,000 in funds being raised, which enabled the successful completion of her project.[33]

These vile acts represented new ways to perpetrate violence against women, and clearly echoed offline violence. Other new forms of harm were also appearing. Doxing (its name derived from 'docs', an abbreviation of 'documents') emerged as a specifically Internet-based practice of researching, and then releasing, personal identifying information online, in an attempt to harass, or encourage others to use the information to harass the victim. Another was the 'online mob'; a particularly aggravating factor of this phenomenon was the anonymity of the harassers, who could, en masse, suffocate online social media accounts and comments sections. In response, women's human rights defenders called for more gendered perspectives on issues of censorship and surveillance.[34]

2.3. A LEGAL REMEDY

A right must have a remedy; something the international human rights system considers so important that a remedy is, in fact, a right in itself.[35]

---

31 P. DEAN, 'Tropes vs. Women in Video Games: Why it Matters', IGN Entertainment, 31.05.2013. Available at <https://www.ign.com/articles/2013/05/31/tropes-vs-women-in-video-games-why-it-matters> accessed 29.04.2020.

32 J. MOOLMAN, above n. 26.

33 ibid. See also <https://www.anitasarkeesian.com>.

34 See, e.g. F. HENSEN, J. KEE, G. VINKITESWARAN and S. RANDHAWA, 'Sexing the Internet: Censorship, Surveillance and the Body Politic(s) of Malaysia' in R. DEIBERT, J. PALFREY, R. ROHOZINSKI and J. ZITTRAIN (eds.), *Access Contested*, The Open Net Initiative, International Development Resource Centre and MIT Press, Cambridge, MA 2011, pp. 65–81.

35 M. FREEMAN and G. VAN ERT, *International Human Rights Law*, Irwin Law Inc., Ontario 2004, pp. 354–57.

A remedy must be justiciable: that is, capable of being determined by a court. Remedies can include financial compensation, rehabilitation, orders to cease or change practices and policies, reinstatement of employment and so on. In the case of Internet interferences, there were significant questions over whether courts could adjudicate over these, and prescribe clear legal remedies capable of holding the duty-bearer accountable for the alleged interference.[36] Internet rights advocates realised that forms of online harm were rapidly evolving, and that these needed appropriate remedies.[37] For example, there were new laws to prevent financial harm from Internet scams (such as 'phishing' activity, designed to steal from unsuspecting or computer-illiterate consumers), or theft of intellectual property by hacking.[38] But remedies for online harm, such as violence against women, were proving elusive.

One particular challenge in finding appropriate remedies was the permanent nature of the Internet. The futility of trying to secure takedown of online content was obvious in Khadija Ismayilova's case, as it proved impossible to identify the source of the video material online; each time a copy was removed, someone would ensure that another one reappeared elsewhere.

Cyberattacks were another case in point. Cyberattacks are attempts to compromise a computer system, for example by hacking into a company's computer network. Many countries have laws against this kind of activity, but new forms of cyberattack were highlighting the absence of remedies for some Internet interferences, such as distributed denial-of-service (DDoS) attacks. There are different types of DDoS attack, but a typical example involves flooding a server with domain name or URL requests.[39] Civil society groups were reporting DDoS attacks which sought to bring down their websites (making them unreachable) to harass and intimidate them,

---

36 See, e.g. K. GLEDHILL, 'The Obligation to Implement and Enforce Human Rights' in M.BEDGGOOD, K. GLEDHILL and I. McINTOSH (eds.), *International Human Rights Law in Aotearoa New Zealand*, Thomson Reuters, Wellington 2017, pp. 233–57, at pp. 247–52.

37 D. LUJAMBIO, F. ROVERI and F. FASCENDINI 'Opportunities and Threats for Internet Rights in Argentina' in *Global Information Society Watch, Special Edition*, Association for Progressive Communications and Hivos, pp. 12–24, at pp. 21–23 <https://www.giswatch.org/2011-update-i-internet-rights-and-democratisation> accessed 03.03.2021.

38 Such laws were relatively simple amendments to criminal codes, for example to ban computer misuse, or unauthorised access to a computer.

39 Cloudflare, 'What is a DDoS Attack', available at <https://www.cloudflare.com/learning/ddos/what-is-a-ddos-attack/> accessed 24.06.2020.

and were convinced that these attacks were being made by governments, or third parties sanctioned by governments. The attacks were often at time-critical moments, such as the day before a public protest, or in the lead-up to a national election.[40] Isolating the origins of this kind of attack was extremely difficult, and identifying the perpetrators even more so.

At the same time, some governments were complaining about groups like Anonymous carrying out DDoS attacks on public websites.[41] Anonymous claimed to be exercising their right to peaceful protest against governments, businesses and law enforcement agencies that it considered to be violating human rights, likening DDoS attacks to the online equivalent of 'sit-ins' blocking access to a building, or stopping traffic on a public road. But such attacks could also prevent innocent citizens from getting access to online government services they needed, putting them at risk, or negatively affect businesses.

Governments, civil society groups and businesses alike might have had their valid suspicions of each other, but obtaining evidence and working out the appropriate remedy (reinstatement of the website, or compensation for business interruption) was very difficult for several reasons.

The first issue was working out where the incident took place, for example was it in the country hosting the website, or was it where the organisation was registered? Depending on the particular country, there might be multiple and conflicting laws, and a range of remedies or none at all. Combatting online censorship might involve litigation based on defamation law, constitutional protections (where these existed), or criminal or civil legislation, depending on the human rights and online activity involved. These jurisdictional issues created significant barriers to the clear identification of possible remedies.

Second, quantifying a remedy needed evidence from technology experts, but depending on the particular country, such experts might simply not exist, or might be difficult to find. Just as difficult was the lack of judges who fully understood how the Internet worked. The nebulous

---

40 H. ROBERTS, E. ZUCKERMAN and J PALFREY, 'Interconnected contests: Distributed Denial of Service Attacks and Other Digital Control Measures in Asia' in R. DEIBERT, J. PALFREY, R. ROHOZINSKI and J. ZITTRAIN (eds.), *Access Contested*, The Open Net Initiative, International Development Resource Centre and MIT Press, Cambridge, MA 2011, pp. 133–51.

41 P. OLSEN, *We Are Anonymous: Inside the Hacker World of Lulzsec, Anonymous, and the Global Cyber Insurgency*, William Heinemann, London 2013. For a brief overview of Anonymous, see also <https://en.wikipedia.org/wiki/Anonymous_(group)> accessed 24.06.2020.

legal environments of many countries, such as the absence of the rule of law, ineffective legal systems, and lack of legislative and constitutional protections, caused difficulties. Conversely, over-regulation and extensive direct or indirect censorship were also causing difficulties.[42]

The diverse human rights situations in different countries added complexity to the actual and perceived limitations of human rights remedies, for example in countries where the government was able to violate human rights with impunity, or where non-state actors were able to act unchecked. For example, in 2012, Amnesty International drew attention to 'credible allegations that businesses were supplying telecommunications technology to authorities in Libya, Iran, China and other governments': equipment which was being used to 'restrict the use of the Internet or to track down users in connection with their involvement in peaceful protests and other activities in violation of their human rights'.[43] While these were serious concerns, there were questions as to the remedies available: could those companies could be sued to prevent them from selling this equipment?

Third, there was the issue of speed: how quickly could a remedy be obtained? Internet activists frequently needed to obtain recourse quickly: in the case of a DDoS attack, within minutes or hours. They were frustrated by the slow and cumbersome nature of most legal processes. The sheer cost of litigation meant that this was simply inaccessible to many individuals and groups, especially as many of the private companies were based in the United States of America. Quick litigation was simply unrealistic.

There were also concerns about new kinds of penalties that were emerging for some online activities. For example, Internet activists were alarmed at proposals for new Internet punishments, such as the French proposal for a 'three strikes' law for intellectual property rights violations, which would result in disconnection from the Internet as a form of punishment.[44] Punitively cutting off Internet access was a very dangerous precedent, since it might be used in other contexts, for example to affect access to education, or other government services, which were increasingly only available online. A related concern was that strategic litigation, or other action to seek remedies for Internet interferences, risked the courts or policymakers introducing new, punitive remedies that would further restrict, rather than secure, Internet access.

---

42 S. KELLY and S.COOK (eds.), *Freedom on the Net: A Global Assessment of Internet and Digital Media*' Freedom House, Washington 2011.

43 Amnesty International, 'Statement to Human Rights Council Panel on Human Rights and the Internet', United Nations, 28 February 2012, A/HRC/19/NGO/121.

44 See discussion in Chapter 2, section 3.5.

Given these complexities, it is no surprise that conceptualising remedies for Internet-related human rights issues was proving difficult, even for the most experienced human rights lawyers. Reflecting on this now, it seems incredible that the definition of a human rights violation on the Internet caused so much difficulty. Yet, at the time, the conceptual and definitional challenges were real and complex, and created significant barriers for traditional human rights lawyers trying to understand the Internet and human rights.

3. IMPLICATIONS FOR ACCOUNTABILITY

The conceptual challenges described above had significant implications for accountability in relation to human rights violations online. The international human rights system is centred on the role of governments, which negotiate and agree on global human rights standards. With governments in control of this international system, human rights advocates naturally focus strongly on the rule of law, the roles and duties of governments to protect and respect human rights of their peoples, the importance of courts in upholding the rule of law, and the role of civil society organisations in matters such as human rights monitoring. In this context, 'governance' focusses on the roles of governments, and their duties to respect, protect, and promote the human rights of all of their citizens. The definition of a human rights violation was critical for those seeking to hold governments accountable for Internet interferences.

The Internet system could hardly be more different to this traditional conception of human rights. The Internet has no single point of control, relying instead upon mutual cooperation among many groups and individuals to operate as a network of networks. Internet standards developed in many different ways, with the simple goal being to 'make a better Internet'. In this context, the rule of law is less important than the binding nature of the concepts that underpin the Internet itself, such as open standards, net neutrality, and consensus based multi-stakeholder rule-making processes.[45] When Internet activists referred to 'Internet governance', they were focussing on the equal but different roles of a wide range of stakeholders, not only governments.

For human rights lawyers like me, this concept of Internet governance was extremely confusing, and I will, unashamedly, confess that it took

---

45 D. SOUTER, above n. 2, p. 13. See also the discussion in Chapter 1, section 2.

me some time to get my head around this fundamentally different kind of 'legal' system. The differences were not only conceptual, but caused very practical problems, such as working out the correct duty-bearer, and the proper remedy to seek. Internet activists, for instance, wanted much more focus on the human rights responsibilities of private sector companies, because these had a variety of critical roles in making the Internet work.

However, international human rights standards that applied to States or governments, did not apply to private companies. Private companies were not members of the UN; only governments were, and while governments might have duties to ensure that private companies did not harm citizens, the primary human rights obligations were incumbent on governments, not the private sector. Important work on the obligations of businesses and human rights by Professor John Ruggie in the United Nations Human Rights Council was underway, which, as we shall see later, was destined to help with the concept of private sector companies as duty-bearers. For most human rights lawyers in 2011, however, the focus on private companies as duty-bearers seemed misplaced.

Conceptual and definitional tensions also flared around Internet access and human rights, with similar difficulties arising from attempts to define an Internet shutdown as a human rights violation. Was there a right to Internet access? If so, who were the rights-holders and duty-bearers? If there was no right to Internet access, what other rights might be relevant? By early 2011, countries such as Estonia, Finland, Greece and Costa Rica had passed laws on Internet access. These laws focused on telecommunications infrastructure for high-quality Internet access, for example setting minimum standards for connectivity quality (such as download or upload speeds). However, to most human rights activists, such laws were rather vague statements of consumer service levels; about as useful as saying that there was a right to the access the telephone or electricity.[46] These did not squarely address the concept of interference with Internet access as a human rights violation.

The technical community also roundly rejected the idea that Internet access could be a human right. In early 2012, for example, Vint Cerf, well known for his role in developing the Internet standard for the Transmission Control Protocol, rejected the idea that the Internet was a human right. Writing in the *New York Times*, Cerf said 'It is a mistake to place any

[46] ibid., p. 23.

particular technology in this exalted category, since over time we will end up valuing the wrong things.'[47]

At the same time, building connectivity infrastructure was critical for Internet activists, and their experiences showed that an open, competitive market had the most potential to ensure lower prices, better quality, and faster connection speeds than closed markets with monopolies.[48] Many developing countries' governments were operating state-run utilities for electricity, water, and gas, but this was changing, as foreign private direct investment, particularly in the telecommunications and ICT sectors, was growing.[49] In countries such as South Africa, for example, Internet activists focussed on the right to Internet access through the lens of ICT sector policy, seeking a competitive market to enable better Internet access.[50]

But ICT sector policy seemed far removed from the daily focus of human rights advocates, and gave rise to suspicions about private sector interests being promoted over human rights. It was one thing to complain about access to the Internet being taken away once it had been provided, as with an Internet shutdown, but worrying about people who did not have Internet access seemed like a privilege of the wealthy, when many of the same people did not have food security, clean water, sanitation services or electricity. Putting the commercial interests of private sector companies ahead of the interests of governments (which relied on their state-run monopolies to generate taxes to fund schools and hospitals) also created suspicion that foreign companies, and the Internet activists who supported them, were trying to destabilise democratic governments to serve their own interests. The politics of access were, shall we say, complicated.

For human rights defenders, arguments about the definition of interferences with the Internet were, ultimately, about who was to be

---

47 V. G. CERF, 'The Internet is not a Human Right', *New York Times*, 04.01.2012 <https://www.nytimes.com/2012/01/05/opinion/internet-access-is-not-a-human-right.html> accessed 03.03.2021.

48 Association for Progressive Communications, 'Perspectives on Universal Free Access to Online Information in South Africa: Free Public Wi-Fi and Zero-rated Content' (Issue Paper), South Africa, September 2017. Available at <https://www.apc.org/en/pubs/perspectives-universal-free-access-online-information-south-africa-free-public-wi-fi-and-zero> accessed 29.04.2020.

49 International Telecommunication Union 'Measuring the Information Society', Geneva 2012, pp. 127–62.

50 Association for Progressive Communications, above n. 48, p. 19.

accountable for human rights violations; a question still asked today in discussions about freedom of expression online.[51] Conversely, for the Internet community, the human rights question had already been answered by how the Internet was designed. Giving effect to human rights standards online seemed very complicated, if not problematic.[52]

51 D. KAYE, *Speech Police: The Global Struggle to Govern the Internet*' Columbia Global Reports, New York 2019, p. 14.

52 D. KORFF, 'The Rule of Law on the Internet and in the Wider Digital World' (Issue Paper), Council of Europe, Commissioner for Human Rights, Strasbourg 2014.

CHAPTER 4
ACCOUNTABILITY FOR HUMAN RIGHTS VIOLATIONS ONLINE

1. INTRODUCTION

Just as the previously described events in the Middle East and North Africa were unfolding, I left my role as a human rights commissioner for a job with the Association for Progressive Communications (APC), focussing on the intersections of the Internet and human rights. I had previously met staff and members of the APC when I attended the Internet Governance Forum (IGF) in Lithuania in 2010. Established in the early 1990s, APC was a network of civil society groups with member organisations in more than 30 countries, doing high quality advocacy and research, and with a solid political stance on Internet issues, especially for women's human rights defenders and human rights in developing countries.[1] Concerned about the new Internet interferences, APC was looking for someone to coordinate their new Connect Your Rights campaign. The campaign was simple: promote Internet rights as human rights, with a focus on the UN human rights system. It was my dream job. The first steps were to review advocacy strategies and regulatory approaches, and devise a plan to develop accountability for Internet-related human rights violations.

2. ADVOCACY STRATEGIES

A campaign like Connect Your Rights campaign[2] needed to respond to the deep conceptual debates about human rights violations that were

---

1 Association for Progressive Communications, *Annual Report 2011*, Johannesburg, 2012, p. 58.

2 Information about the Connect Your Rights: Internet Rights are Human Rights campaign, which was funded by the Swedish International Development Agency, is

making it difficult to find accountability for interferences with the Internet, in the international human rights system. APC was documenting the trends in such interferences with the Internet, and did not like what it saw. Restricting freedom of expression, freedom of association, and the free flow of information had become a global trend, and its impact was being felt most in countries that lacked a culture of democracy or a strong human rights regime. Combatting this trend needed new strategies: ones that could build on the communication rights movement, and the related advocacy strategies that grew out of the early days of Internet governance.

2.1. ADVOCATING FOR 'COMMUNICATION RIGHTS'

Consideration of human rights in the context of new media began in the 1960s. Then, Jean d'Arcy, a UN official, was considering the implications of satellite broadcasting and other new media, and proposed the 'right to communicate' as a way to give effect to the Universal Declaration of Human Rights (UDHR) in a global communications context. In so doing, d'Arcy attempted to add to, rather than replace, existing human rights standards.[3] D'Arcy believed that traditional rights were based on outdated assumptions of individual communication, with the result that the related focus on how information was distributed, such as through mass media, was also outdated. Instead, a right to communicate was seen as a better approach to regulating the media, encapsulating both the notion of individual and collective rights (such as the rights to language and to culture), and as leverage for citizens to demand state action, rather than simply acting as a shield against state interference with media activities. There was considerable promise in this new way of thinking about communication rights, and d'Arcy's work held considerable promise for understanding the human rights implications of new technologies.

However, even by the 1980s, communication rights were struggling to gain traction, for various reasons, mainly related to the geopolitics of broadcasting and news media ownership.[4] But Internet activists had

available at <https://www.apc.org/en/projects/internet-rights-are-human-rights> accessed 04.03.2021.

3 For a useful overview of the development of communication rights, see D. MAC SÍTHIGH, 'From Freedom of Speech to the Right to Communicate' in M. E. PRICE, S. VERHULST and L. MORGAN (eds.), *Routledge Handbook of Media Law*, Routledge, London 2013, pp. 174–91.

4 See, e.g. D. HICKS 'The Right to Communicate: Past Mistakes and Future Possibilities' (2007) 3 *Dalhousie Journal of Information and Management*, p. 3.

picked up the concept of communication rights in the 1990s, by which time a broad and diverse range of individuals and groups interested in the Internet had emerged, each articulating their own concepts of human rights and Internet, and each driven by concerns about different kinds of social injustice. In the early 2000s, a new movement emerged around the concept, with calls for the right to communicate as a response to the development of the Internet.[5] The rise in popularity of the concept is obvious from the documents of the World Summit on the Information Society, held in 2003 and 2005.[6]

Communication rights were a particularly useful focus for engaging these diverse groups on Internet access, and the infrastructural issues in developing countries that were affecting the access to telecommunications there.[7] In many African countries, for example, state-run telecommunications monopolies were charging high prices for telephone-based communications, including fax transmissions on phone lines. Internet communication was a faster, cheaper way to communicate, but governments in the region were wary of it, partly because it was being promoted by North American corporations, and partly because of potential losses in the tax revenue state-run monopolies created, revenue that was needed for public spending, such as health and education. The subject of communication rights, therefore, encapsulated concerns about the need for public access to telecommunications infrastructure, as well as concerns about protecting public dialogue from interference by corporate media monopolies.

The 'right to communicate' was also considered a clearer and more direct way of encapsulating the duties of governments to respect and protect rights and freedoms relevant to telecommunications infrastructure. The rights to freedom from unreasonable search and seizure, and to freedom of expression, did not seem adequate to encompass, for example, a government's responsibility to prevent an Internet shutdown. A right to communicate, on the other hand, could be more easily linked to telecommunications infrastructure regulation and an obligation to keep

---

5 W. McIVER, W. BIRDSALL and M. RASMUSSEN, 'The Internet and the Right to Communicate' (2003) *First Monday*, 8 (12) <https://doi.org/10.5210/fm.v8i12.1102> accessed 14.06.2020.

6 D. MAC SÍTHIGH, above n. 3; and see also P. CHAKRAVARTTY, 'Governance Without Politics: Civil Society, Development and the Postcolonial State' (2007) *International Journal of Communication*, 1 (2007) 297–317, 304.

7 D. MAC SÍTHIGH, above n. 3, p. 185.

the Internet working.[8] As the 'right to communicate' movement grew, diverse Internet community stakeholders began to focus their advocacy strategies on the drafting of Internet Bills of Rights as a way to articulate the right to communicate online.

2.2. ADVOCATING FOR CHARTERS OF INTERNET RIGHTS AND PRINCIPLES

One hallmark of advocacy strategies in the early part of the twenty-first century was the rise of Internet charters, declarations, or Bills of Rights. Declarations of Internet rights or principles began as a trickle and became a tidal wave. Similarly to the way in which new declarations of principles and ethics to guide artificial intelligence have recently emerged (as will be examined in Chapter 8), these initiatives seemed to flow in several different directions.

In one direction were the advocacy strategies of civil society groups, who used multi-stakeholder processes, similar to those used to develop Internet Protocols, to develop declarations of Internet rights and principles. Such declarations largely articulated the UDHR as it applied to the Internet. The APC Charter of Internet Rights, for example, affirmed the UDHR, defining its application in online contexts, including freedom from censorship, the right to online organising and protest, and the freedom to express opinions and ideas when using the Internet.[9] The Charter of Human Rights and Principles for the Internet, developed by the Internet Governance Forum's Internet Rights and Principles Dynamic Coalition, similarly included the freedom to protest, freedom from censorship, the right to information, and the freedom of the media.[10] The latter charter also referred to the right to 'form, join, meet or visit the website or network of an assembly, group, or association for any reason' and called for access to assemblies and associations using information communication technologies (ICTs) not to be blocked or filtered.[11] Such charters

8 ibid., p. 184–86.

9 Association for Progressive Communications, 'Internet Rights Charter', 2006 <https://www.apc.org/en/pubs/about-apc/apc-internet-rights-charter> accessed 04.03.2021.

10 Internet Rights and Principles Dynamic Coalition, UN Internet Governance Forum, 'The Charter of Human Rights and Principles for the Internet', 2010, available at <https://www.internetrightsandprinciples.org> accessed 04.03.2021.

11 ibid., Article 7.

were generally very comprehensive, but some were also condensed into simpler sets of principles.[12]

These efforts included restatement of the UDHR in Internet-related ways, as well as the framing of new rights relating specifically to communication rights concepts, for example the right to share, and the right to copy. Others focussed on specific rights, such as privacy (the Madrid Privacy Declaration),[13] or particular online users (the Bill of Privacy Rights for Social Network Users).[14]

Campaigns on Internet access, net neutrality, free culture, and access to knowledge took place in many countries, and some advocacy strategies were so successful that they achieved law changes. The Charter for Innovation, Creativity and Access to Knowledge of 2009, for example, developed by a coalition from more than 20 countries, was used to negotiate new laws with the Spanish government, and was presented to the European Council.[15] New Estonian law also referenced access to the Internet as a right.[16] In Norway, the government issued regulations for the telecommunications sector on Internet network neutrality which provided that 'Internet users are entitled to an Internet connection that is free of discrimination with regard to type of application, service or content or based on sender or receiver address.'[17]

At the same time, private sector advocacy strategies were also emerging. Such efforts were new, since the private sector had traditionally shied away from direct engagement with the international human rights system (with the main exceptions being in aspects of employment and working conditions). Increasingly concerned about requests from governments and

---

12 For example, Internet Rights and Principles Dynamic Coalition, UN Internet Governance Forum, '10 Internet Rights and Principles', 2011 <https://internetrightsandprinciples.org/charter/> accessed 04.03.2021.

13 'The Madrid Privacy Declaration: Global Privacy Standards for a Global World', 03.09.2009, available at <https://thepublicvoice.org/madrid-declaration/> accessed 14.06.2020.

14 K. OPSAHL, 'A Bill of Privacy Rights for Social Network Users', Electronic Frontier Foundation, 19.05.2010, available at <http://www.eff.org/deeplinks/2010/05/bill-privacy-rights-social-network-users> accessed 14.06.2020.

15 The Charter for Creativity, Innovation and Knowledge was developed by the Free Culture Forum in November 2009, <https://2009.fcforum.net/en/> accessed 04.03.2021.

16 C. WOODARD, 'Estonia, Where Being Wired is a Human Right', *Christian Science Monitor*, 01.07.2003 <https://www.csmonitor.com/2003/0701/p07s01-woeu.html> accessed 04.03.2021.

17 Norwegian Post and Telecommunications, 'Network Neutrality: Guidelines for Internet Neutrality', Post-og Teletilsynet, version 1.0, 24.02.2009.

law enforcement agencies for Internet shutdowns or online surveillance, and the resulting public backlash against them, some private sector corporations formed alliances with civil society groups, or collaborated to form their own 'coalitions of the willing'– business groups prepared to talk about, or even be accountable for, the human rights effects of their actions.

An initial focus was on the repudiation of requests to companies from law enforcement agencies without a court order; for example, to Internet service providers for details of the email accounts of human rights defenders, or to close down Facebook profiles that did not comply with company rules. This developed into transparency reporting, whereby corporations would publish information about the number of requests they had received in their annual reports. Google, for example, published its first transparency report in 2010 and others, such as Twitter and Facebook, followed.[18] Other initiatives used multi-stakeholder processes to develop their policy positions on human rights. The Global Network Initiative, for example, was formed by 'companies, investors, civil society organizations and academics' who subscribed to the Global Network Initiative Principles, and focussed on freedom of expression and privacy.[19]

Some of these private sector advocacy strategies were formulated within the UN itself. The UN Global Compact, for example, established in 2000, aimed to support companies to align with human rights through voluntary CEO commitments.[20] The Compact developed ten principles focused on labour, anti-corruption and environmental rights,[21] but it did not engage with those focused on communication rights.[22] Finally, Silicon Valley also got in on the act, hosting a Silicon Valley Human Rights Summit (Rightscon) in 2011, one of the few successful private sector initiatives that still has high participation rates today.[23]

---

18 Google Inc., 'Google Transparency Report', 2010 <https://transparencyreport.google.com/> accessed 04.03.2021; and, for a useful summary of trends, see Access Now, 'Transparency Reporting Index' available at <https://www.accessnow.org/transparency-reporting-index/> accessed 04.03.2021.

19 Global Network Initiative, 'The Global Network Initiative Principles on Freedom of Expression and Privacy', 2008, available at <https://globalnetworkinitiative.org/gni-principles/> accessed 14.06.2020.

20 United Nations, The UN Global Compact <https://www.unglobalcompact.org> accessed 04.03.2021.

21 United Nations, The Ten Principles of the UN Global Compact <https://www.unglobalcompact.org/what-is-gc/mission/principles> accessed 04.03.2021.

22 See UN Global Compact participant list <https://www.unglobalcompact.org> accessed 14.06.2020.

23 Rightscon is organised by Access Now. See <https://www.rightscon.org/about-and-contact/> and, for the first Rightscon, see Electronic Frontier Foundation, 'Guide to

Increasingly alarmed by the rapidly forming online platform monopolies that appeared to have more power than some nation states, intergovernmental organisations responded to these advocacy strategies by developing their own positions on human rights and the Internet. The Council of Europe, the Organisation for Economic Co-operation and Development (OECD), and many others, negotiated their own statements of principles about Internet governance for states to follow when developing Internet-related regulation and policy.[24] In 2011, for example, the OECD released a communiqué on principles for Internet policymaking,[25] developed with the help of its internal Civil Society Information Society Advisory Council. Civil society members, however, backed away from the final draft, refusing to endorse the communiqué, on the grounds that its proposed intellectual property clauses could undermine 'online freedom of expression, freedom of information, the right to privacy, [and] access to knowledge and innovation across the world'.[26] Although not a total failure, it was clear that civil society's advocacy influence was still limited; dependent on governments willing to listen to, and represent, its views in internal negotiations. Creating the kinds of open processes used by the Internet community, in which negotiating power was more equally distributed among stakeholders, was a long way off.

Finally, advocacy strategies focussing on national-level initiatives were also developing, perhaps the most well known and successful of which was Brazil's Marco de Civil, or national law on the 'Framework for the Internet'.[27] This law was the culmination of a partnership between the Ministry of Justice and the Centre for Technology and Society in the Law Faculty of Fundação Getúlio Vargas, and developed through a series of national consultations between 2009 and 2012. Both the law and the process of developing it were unique, with the technical community deeply involved; it used an approach that seemed to bridge the complexities and conceptual challenges that plagued others. The Bill itself

Rightscon', 2011, available at <https://www.eff.org/deeplinks/2011/10/eff-guide-to-rightscon> accessed 24.06.2020.

24 Council of Europe, 'Declaration by the Committee of Ministers on Internet Governance Principles', Brussels, 21.09.2011.

25 OECD, 'Communiqué on Principles for Internet Policy Making', Paris, 28/29.06.2011.

26 Association for Progressive Communications, above n. 1.

27 For a comprehensive overview, see L. MONCAU and D. ARGUELHES, 'Marco de Civil da Internet and Digital Constitutionalism' in G. FROSIO (ed.), *Oxford Handbook of Online Intermediary Liability*, Oxford University Press, Oxford 2020, pp. 190–213. An English translation by Carolina Rossini (April 2014) is available at <https://www.publicknowledge.org/documents/marco-civil-english-version/> accessed 04.03.2021.

proposed Internet access as a fundamental prerequisite for other rights, emphasised net neutrality, and proposed safe harbours for Internet service providers. The law was eventually passed in 2013, in reaction to news of the United States' NSA surveillance of Brazilian telecommunications networks.[28]

2.3. ADVOCATING FOR A RIGHTS-BASED APPROACH TO HUMAN RIGHTS AND THE INTERNET

Another, softer advocacy strategy was the rights-based approach, or human rights approach. First articulated in 2002, the rights-based approach developed as a practical way to implement human rights standards when the Office of the UN High Commissioner for Human Rights convened an ad hoc expert committee on biotechnology. Biotechnology was a new, and still emerging, area of human rights, with no specific human rights standards. To overcome some of the conceptual difficulties in applying human rights standards, the committee decided to adopt a 'rights-based approach' for its task, indicating that such an approach should:[29]

- emphasise the participation of individuals in decision making;
- introduce accountability for actions and decisions, which can allow individuals to complain about decisions affecting them adversely;
- seek non-discrimination of all individuals through the equal application of rights and obligations to all individuals;
- empower individuals by allowing them to use rights as a leverage for action, and to legitimise their voice in decision-making; and
- link decision-making at every level to the agreed international human rights norms in the various human rights covenants and treaties.

This approach was seen as very useful, and was picked up in a wide range of areas in the UN, particularly those where no specific human rights standards seemed to apply, or those which were politically sensitive. For example, the Special Representative for Business and Human Rights,

[28] A. MARI, '"Internet Constitution" becomes a priority for Brazilian Government', 10.07.2013, available at <https://www.zdnet.com/article/internet-constitution-becomes-priority-for-brazilian-government/> accessed 12.06.2020.

[29] Office of the High Commissioner for Human Rights, 'Report of the High Commissioner's Expert Group on Human Rights and Biotechnology: Conclusions', 2002, Geneva, para. 21.

Professor John Ruggie, drew on the rights-based approach when considering the liability of transnational corporations for human rights violations. Ruggie's work was important because it responded to the conceptual problem of the place of corporates as duty bearers in international human rights. Drawing on the rights-based approach, Ruggie developed a new framework for businesses to respect, protect and remedy human rights that emphasised the need for access to effective remedies, both judicial and non-judicial, for corporate actions that violate human rights.[30]

Civil society groups also used the approach, for example to analyse the likely effects of proposed Internet regulations on access to the Internet, privacy, and filtering,[31] and to criticise regulation of the mobile Internet.[32] Although the approach was useful, and there was plenty of scope to use it in some areas, for example in thinking about Internet governance, it was more of an analytical tool than an advocacy strategy.

2.4. ADVOCACY STRATEGIES AND NATIONAL HUMAN RIGHTS INSTITUTIONS

National human rights institutions such as ombudsmen, data protection or privacy agencies, and human rights commissions were not universally engaged with communications rights or complaints of Internet interferences. In 2011, for example, of the three regional human rights bodies, only the European Court of Human Rights was receiving an increasing number of strategic complaints and related interventions in litigation by civil society groups.[33] There was little activity in the Inter-American Court of Human Rights or the African Court on Human and Peoples' Rights. There had been no complaints to the African Special Rapporteur on Freedom of

30 J. RUGGIE, 'Report of the Special Representative of the Secretary-General on the Issue of Human Rights and Transnational Corporations and other Business Enterprises' and 'Guiding Principles on Business and Human Rights: Implementing the United Nations "Protect, Respect and Remedy" Framework', 21 March 2011, A/HRC/17/31, paras. 26–31.

31 Access Now, 'To Regulate or Not to Regulate, is that the Question? A Roadmap to Smart Regulation of the Internet', discussion paper released ahead of the OECD High-Level Meeting on the Internet Economy, 28 and 29.06.2011.

32 See, e.g. L. HORNER, 'A Human Rights Approach to the Mobile Internet' (Issue Paper, May 2011), Association for Progressive Communications <www.apc.org> accessed 12.06.2020.

33 European Court of Human Rights, 'Summary of European Court of Human Rights Cases in Relation to the Internet and Human Rights' (New Technologies Fact Sheet), May 2011.

Expression and Access to Information in relation to freedom of expression and the Internet.[34] There were a small number of significant complaints to national human rights institutions, such as in South Korea,[35] but my experience in New Zealand was that, generally, such institutions simply had not considered how to deal with the Internet, or Internet-related complaints.

Given these complexities, it is perhaps surprising that those advocating for communication rights, or seeking to raise concerns about human rights and the Internet, largely steered away from suggesting new accountability mechanisms such as new courts or tribunals. After all, if the existing mechanisms were not effective, surely it would be best to create new ones, tailored to the Internet? There were calls for special Internet courts in a few areas, for example in relation to hearing complaints about bloggers and other non-traditional forms of press, as well as radio and television media. But, in general, new 'Internet courts' were shied away from for several reasons. Various conceptual challenges made determining the appropriate role of any new courts very hard (for instance, over which parts of the Internet would there be jurisdiction? And in which country, and how, would judgments be enforced?). The risk was very high that, without proper technical expertise, judges in both existing and new courts would simply lack the requisite expertise and, in any event, many countries' legal systems were already overwhelmed with existing cases. Advocacy strategies, therefore, generally steered away from creating new tribunals or other accountability forums.

Just as civil society groups, the private sector, and other stakeholders were developing advocacy strategies, governments were developing a range of regulatory approaches in their roles as duty-bearers, responsible for respecting and protecting human rights, and this will be discussed in the following section.

3. REGULATORY APPROACHES

As outlined in Chapter 1, many of the evolutionary 'Big Bang' developments of the Internet happened without Internet-specific laws

34 Advocate Pansy Tsakula, personal communication to Association for Progressive Communications, 2011.

35 The Korean Progressive Network Jinbonet continues to be very active in the Human Rights Council and related mechanisms. See <https://act.jinbo.net/wp/p22028/page/2/> accessed 02.12.2020.

or regulations: the emergence of new Internet Protocols, Internet exchange points, applications, and devices such as the laptop and mobile phone – all happened largely within existing regulatory frameworks. While these frameworks were not wholly problematic, some gaps definitely began to emerge, and the global nature of the Internet presented conceptual and other difficulties for existing models of governance and law. Governments were diverging on whether, and how, to respond to these difficulties, their respective directions seemingly influenced by deeply held views about their roles.

In one direction were those favouring 'permission-less innovation', the concept that there should be no barriers – no limits – to opportunities to create and innovate.[36] Policymakers going in this direction favoured no new rules, and even the removal of some existing rules regulating the Internet or online content, seeing the role of governments as being to protect their citizens by staying out of their way.

Those favouring the 'precautionary principle' went in another direction, supporting the concept that creation and innovation should do no harm, and that regulation would be a driver of responsible technology development. Policymakers from this school of thought saw the role of governments as being to protect their citizens by intervening, with regulation, to prevent or minimise harm.[37]

Then there was the 'technological solutionism' or 'technological determinism' direction: the idea that technology simply reflected society and the related idea that there was no 'good' or 'bad' technologies, only bad actors, so technology developers should simply be trusted to deliver beneficial results. These adherents had an almost evangelical fervour towards the Internet as the solution to many problems, with some countries competing to be the fastest, easiest or cheapest place to deploy or develop new technologies: to be the next Silicon Valley.[38]

Finally, there were those favouring regulatory intervention to evenly distribute the 'digital dividends' of the Internet, seeing the role of governments as being to reduce existing inequalities, and avoid the new ones that were already emerging from 'digital divides' between men and

---

36 By way of explanation, see, e.g. A. THIERER, *Permissionless Innovation: The Continuing Case for Comprehensive Technological Freedom*, Mercatus Center, George Mason University, Virginia 2016, pp. 8–15.

37 ibid., pp. 23–29.

38 For a useful overview, see D. SOUTER (ed.), 'ICT Policy Handbook', Association for Progressive Communications, 2009.

women, young and old, and between the developed Global North and developing Global South.[39]

These various directions, and others, generated a lot of debate. Some considered that the absence of regulatory limits enabled companies to act with impunity, and was out of step with the approach in many other sectors where the precautionary approach worked well, such as pharmaceuticals and consumer goods. The consequences of lack of regulation could be disastrous, as seen in the global financial crisis, the use of lead in petrol and asbestos in construction, and even child labour and modern forms of slavery. The idea that rules would stifle innovation was a myth: after all, most sports are better because there are rules. There was too much faith being put in 'permissionless innovation': democratic processes, it was argued, made better policy than unregulated ones.[40]

But others strongly argued for 'permissionless innovation', particularly to protect the technical Internet community and their standards-making processes from interference by governments. The Internet community was focussed on making the Internet the best it could be, and did not want policymakers, however well-intentioned, interfering. Policy experts, in turn, argued that all decisions, technical or not, had policy implications, and that the distinction between 'technical' and 'policy' issues was a spurious one.[41]

At the same time, many governments were also beginning to grapple with the challenges of regulating converging technologies: the telecommunications, broadcasting and communications sectors were coming together. Some of these, such as telephones and broadcasting, had existing regulators. Some, such as the Internet, did not.[42] One purpose of regulation was oversight of competitive markets, but this was quite different to content regulation in broadcasting. Policymakers were unclear how, if at all, these sectors could or should be brought together. With little experience in the Internet, most governments and intergovernmental organisations 'were poorly placed to influence its direction or to integrate internet standards and behaviour into national and international law'.[43] Many were genuinely struggling with how to adapt and find the best policy approaches.

---

39 ibid.
40 ibid., pp. 138–42.
41 ibid.
42 D. SOUTER, above n. 38, pp. 104–05.
43 ibid., p. 138.

4. FROM COMMUNICATION RIGHTS TO INTERNET RIGHTS

Advocacy for communication rights gained currency in those parts of the UN that were already Internet governance-focussed, such as the Commission on Science and Technology for Development, which was discussing improvements to the IGF. In other parts of the UN, discussion about communication rights was largely absent. Given the level of focus on Internet governance and communication rights elsewhere, it was remarkable how little attention the Internet was getting from the international human rights system. It is still surprising that, by early 2011, there had been only three resolutions in the Human Rights Council that mentioned the Internet in any substantive way. To my relatively fresh eyes, it seemed as if governments and civil society alike were deliberately avoiding the topic. There may be some truth to that, but in reality it is more likely that a variety of factors were contributing to this absence of discussion: competing priorities, lack of awareness, and lack of need. After all, the Internet was working perfectly well without UN or governmental action.

The significant exception was women's human rights. As discussed in Chapter 3, women's human rights defenders around the world paid attention to issues of violence against women, and portrayal of women and girls in the media, and were worried about women's access to ICTs, and the emergence of new forms of violence online. In 1995, women's rights defenders stole a march, on Internet and human rights, by persuading governments to refer to ICTs, including Internet access, in the agreements about women's rights and the media.[44]

There were also a few green shoots of discussion about civil and political rights and the Internet. In 2010, for example, the UN Human Rights Committee began a review of General Comment no. 34 (a key document used to interpret the meaning of the right to freedom of expression contained in Article 19 of the International Covenant on Civil and Political Rights). The Committee's preliminary report, finalised in July 2011, proposed a new General Comment with specific reference to 'electronic and Internet-based modes of expression'.[45] This was a welcome development, as it would

---

[44] Beijing Platform for Action, Section J paras. 234 and 237, available at <https://www.un.org/womenwatch/daw/beijing/platform/media.htm> accessed 05.03.2021.

[45] Human Rights Committee, 'Draft General Comment no. 34' (upon completion of the first reading by the Human Rights Council), CCPR/C/GC/34/CRP.6, 03.05.2011, para. 11.

strengthen the hand of civil society groups wanting recourse for, and an avenue for reporting, Internet-related violations of freedom of expression under Article 19. But, overall, there was little substantive engagement within human rights bodies on the subject of communication rights.

The picture that emerges is mixed. On the one hand, there were many criticisms of advocacy for charters and principles on Internet rights. For example, none of these contained new types of complaints procedures, leaving newly articulated rights without a remedy. Without clear legal mandates, and enforcement mechanisms of some kind, these declarations could only ever be aspirational statements from various informal groups. While their intentions were good, there was also no imperative to use the new charters and principles. So, over time, the enthusiasm for declarations as tools for effective advocacy and action began to wane. Participation, and being seen to be involved, became more important than meaningful action to uphold rights, and there were concerns that challenging wrongful acts of the private sector or governments by 'calling these out' during negotiations was putting consensus at risk. Ultimately, the advocacy strategy of a call to 'communication rights' was not enough. 'Consensus building' was becoming something akin to singing to the choir. By the end of 2010, attempts to garner support for these new charters, as an advocacy strategy, was foundering, and they eventually stalled.[46]

Despite this, advocacy for Internet rights and principles did serve some important purposes. Each involved consultation processes, and those processes enabled more education and advocacy, increasing the number of people aware of the issues and willing to share their experiences. The sheer volume of initiatives probably meant it was inevitable that a global movement for change would develop, along with discussions about whether a global charter might emerge, or whether a new global treaty was needed.

Some of the initiatives also made significant contributions to increasing the awareness of Internet interferences, and new activists, groups, and even political parties emerged. There were the Pirate Parties, born from opposition to intellectual property laws, of which Iceland's Pirate Party was the most successful, securing more than 16 per cent of the vote in national elections in 2016.[47] There were other, much less successful parties, such as

46 D. HAWTIN, 'Internet Charters and Principles: Trends and Insights' in *Global Information Society Watch*, Association for Progressive Communications and Hivos, 2011, pp. 51–54 <https://www.giswatch.org/en/2011> accessed 05.03.2021.

47 The Icelandic Pirate Party <https://piratar.is/english/> accessed 05.03.2021.

the Internet Party, founded by Kim Dotcom in New Zealand to contest the 2014 election.[48]

As awareness grew, and more people became involved, academics, lawyers and human rights defenders studied the issues more closely, and gained deeper insights into the Internet interferences that were occurring within the wide cracks in the existing human rights framework. Advocacy for communication rights and Internet Bills of Rights was an excellent way to bring these injustices to the fore, highlight bad actors, and bring worldwide attention to the plight of ordinary people in far-flung corners of the globe.

The negotiation of charters and principles also, inevitably, involved discussion and agreement on how different rights and freedoms worked together. In the offline world, human rights violations may involve multiple and intersecting rights across different rights frameworks (freedom of expression, the right to development, freedom from violence and harassment) and groups (such as women, sexual and gender minorities, people with disabilities, or racial and cultural minorities). The rights-based approach was one way to reconcile these conflicting or competing rights, and to take account of the effects on different groups.

However, the question of conflicting or competing rights gave rise to further difficult questions and conversations for those developing Internet Bills of Rights, since the negotiation of charters and principles inevitably involved discussion, and agreement, on how different rights and freedoms worked together and affected different groups. What was the scope of the rights and freedoms to be included? Were all rights to be treated the same, or were some, such as first-generation rights like freedom of expression, more important than second-generation rights like the right to health? Where did that leave third-generation rights like communication rights?

New rights and freedoms were struggling to be accommodated amongst tangled interpretations of human rights law: was the right to *seek, receive and impart information of any kind in any form* tantamount to a right to share information online? Even if it was, then, given that the rights and freedoms were not absolute, what limitations on such a right would be reasonable? What about the harmful effects that some online speech had on the non-discrimination rights of minorities, or the application of hate speech laws to the Internet? How did this sit alongside the view that the Internet should be open, and all traffic travel freely? How would an Internet Bill of Rights resolve these kinds of conflict? Such discussions

48 The Internet Party <https://www.internet.org.nz> accessed 05.03.2021.

laid critical foundations for resolving some of the conceptual difficulties of whether, and how, an Internet interference might fall within the definition of a human rights violation.

Another advocacy challenge was how to ensure that all of the new Internet-related human rights issues were covered by the concept of communication rights. Such issues ranged from the production lines of ICT manufacturers (conflict minerals, the rights of workers, or trade-related issues), to surveillance, content filtering, content blocking, harassment, and the arrest and detention of online human rights activists. It seemed difficult to find a single, coherent way to frame these human rights issues in an online context. The sheer speed of technological developments was also making it difficult to develop an agreed application of human rights standards to fast-changing forms of connectivity, particularly as mobile connectivity was beginning to outpace the desktop computer and other forms of connectivity. This also posed significant challenges to developing clear advocacy strategies.

By the end of 2010, the organising force of these initiatives was on the wane, energy was low, and some were documenting 'charter overload'.[49] The myriad of principles and campaign initiatives was becoming exhausting to participate in and follow. Civil society groups were both supportive of each other's efforts and competitive about their own respective campaigns. The number and diversity of these groups enabled some 'forum shopping' or 'rights shopping', and alliances formed around which charter initiative seemed to serve one set of multi-stakeholder interests over another.

In short, communication rights were an important and useful framework for advocacy strategies and, by the early 2010s, had resulted in many significant achievements. But, as new forms of interference with the Internet emerged in the mid to late 2010s, communication rights were not enough to protect the full range of rights and freedoms that were coming under attack. Attacks on freedom of association, harassment and detention of bloggers and journalists, and surveillance and harassment of women's rights defenders had become global trends. These issues went much deeper than communication rights relating to new forms of media, and access to public information. Charters of Internet rights would not disappear completely, and some, such as the African Declaration on Internet Rights and Freedoms,[50] would be effective organising and advocacy tools.

---

49 D. HAWTIN, above n. 46.

50 African Declaration on Internet Rights and Freedoms, Johannesburg, 2014 <https://africaninternetrights.org/declaration/> accessed 01.02.2021.

However, a more comprehensive Internet and human rights advocacy strategy was needed. The APC's Connect Your Rights campaign was one attempt to respond to this changing context, by focussing on Internet rights more generally.

5. AN ADVOCACY STRATEGY FOR THE HRC

My first tasks after joining the APC were to support the upcoming presentation of the annual report of the Special Rapporteur on Freedom of Opinion and Expression, coordinate an event in the halls of the UN, and figure out a way to bring the stories of activists into the Human Rights Council (HRC). To achieve this, Connect Your Rights had four broad strategies.[51]

Firstly, to talk in a language that human rights experts could understand, by finding ways to describe Internet experiences in human rights terms. Was a state-sponsored DDoS attack of an NGO website an interference with freedom of expression or freedom of association? Was online circulation of fake sexually explicit images containing the faces of women human rights defenders the same as sexual harassment offline? In short, the focus was on finding ways to advocate for human rights online using much clearer articulation of real-life experiences, but in existing human rights language.

Secondly, to connect the concepts of human rights and the Internet by directly, and very powerfully, linking the effects of interferences with Internet access (such as Internet shutdowns) with negative effects on other rights, such as the rights to democratic participation, freedom of association, and freedom from discrimination. This nexus between online and offline rights and freedoms was critical. People were much more likely to understand human rights and the Internet if they could see how this related to their concerns about police harassment, arrest and detention of journalists, security, or violence against women. The aim was to show the negative effects on civil and political rights with specific examples, such as email interceptions without warrants, detentions for Twitter comments, and kidnappings of women, enabled by the use of unlawfully accessed location data.

Thirdly, to build the capacity of those using Internet technology to defend themselves from interferences, and develop campaigns to educate

51 See also Association for Progressive Communications, 'Connect Your Rights: Internet Rights are Human Rights Campaign' 16.11.2011 <https://www.apc.org/en/projects/internet-rights-are-human-rights> accessed 05.03.2021.

communities about the emerging issues; to help build movements, extend networks, and encourage engagement with the issues among those more familiar with human rights.

Fourthly, to demand accountability for the illegal activities of governments and private or non-state actors. Framing Internet interferences as human rights violations, for which governments were already accountable, would engage the international human rights system, and enable investigations and the use of complaints processes.

It was also necessary to address several other factors affecting why the Internet was not really a focus of human rights in the UN. One was the lack of engagement with the Internet by most civil society groups. The United Nations had accredited thousands of organisations which focussed either on particular human rights issues (such as racism, privacy, armed conflict or the right to development) or particular groups (children, indigenous peoples, women and girls, or disabled people). Many submitted monitoring reports to the various UN human rights mechanisms and treaty bodies, and participated in human rights proceedings and other events to highlight their concerns. These reports documented human rights violations, made recommendations to governments, and asked treaty bodies to examine and publicly question government actions.

By early 2011, only a handful of these thousands of organisations had specifically commented on the Internet and human rights at the HRC. Those that had were mainly groups already focussed on protecting journalists (such as Reporters Sans Frontières), whose concerns had spread to the Internet as existing news media journalists moved online and a new kind of citizen journalist, the blogger, emerged. In 2009, for example, the Egyptian and American governments co-sponsored a resolution on freedom of opinion and expression which recognised the importance of 'all forms of the media including … the Internet' and called on states to 'facilitate equal participation in, access to and use of information communication technology, such as the Internet'.[52] Just a handful of groups working on Internet issues were reporting on their specific country (such as Jinbonet, focused on South Korea),[53] or more generally on Internet freedom.[54]

52 UN Human Rights Council Resolution 12/16 on Freedom of Expression and Opinion (12 October 2009) A/HRC/RES/12/16, available at <https://www.right-docs.org/doc/a-hrc-res-12-16/> accessed 05.03.2021.

53 Association for Progressive Communications, 'Hyper-connected South Koreans Face Shrinking Internet Freedom, says UN', 28.05.2011 <https://www.apc.org/en/node/10498> accessed 05.03.2021.

54 Freedom House, for example, produced annual reports on Internet freedom: see <https://www.freedomhouse.org> accessed 05.03.2021 and, more generally, see

There were very practical reasons for the lack of Internet and human rights focus: most mainstream human rights groups were still not using new technologies for their work. Many did not have an online social media presence beyond simple websites, in part because they did not receive funding for it.

Another factor, partly reflecting lack of civil society engagement, was the small number of human rights resolutions. What few there were of these tended to be very general, focussed on the rights of journalists, and reiterating the importance of the free flow of ideas.[55]

Taking a campaign into the UN human rights system is daunting. Yet, for all its many imperfections, the HRC was the only global human rights forum. We had to consider advocacy strategies and find opportunities for recourse against states; ways to hold them accountable for human rights violations, taking into account the strengths and limitations of each option. I canvassed the existing processes: treaty bodies, complaints under optional protocols, engagement with the individual Special Procedures (for example, the Special Rapporteurs for Freedom of Opinion and Expression, Freedom of Association, and Human Rights Defenders), and the newly developed state peer-to-peer Universal Periodic Review process.[56]

In 2010, the Special Rapporteur on Freedom of Opinion and Expression, Frank La Rue, decided to focus his next annual report on the Internet. This decision followed a reference to the Internet in the resolution sponsored by Sweden the previous year. La Rue, a Guatemalan lawyer and human rights expert, had been forced to live in exile after serving as legal adviser to the Central General de Trabajadores de Guatemala, the nation's largest trade union, subsequently returning to co-found the Center for Legal Action for Human Rights in 1990.[57] La Rue was also blind, and a strong advocate for the rights of people with disabilities. APC participated in a series of consultations in Asia, Latin America, Europe, Africa and North America in 2009 and 2010, where La Rue had been documenting a wide range of interferences with the Internet. He planned to present his findings in his 2011 annual report to the HRC.[58] This would be the first detailed effort by

J. LIDDICOAT 'Human Rights Online: New Issues and Threats' (Issues Paper), Association for Progressive Communications (2011) <https://www.apc.org/en/pubs/issue/policy/human-rights-online-new-issues-and-threats> accessed 05.03.2021.

55 Above n. 52.

56 The Universal Periodic Review process is discussed in more detail in Chapter 5.

57 See <https://en.wikipedia.org/wiki/Frank_William_La_Rue> accessed 04.03.2021.

58 F. LA RUE, United Nations Human Rights Council, 'Report of the Special Rapporteur on the Promotion and Protection of the Right to Freedom of Opinion and Expression' (A/HRC/17/27) 26.04.2011.

a UN human rights expert to frame the Internet in human rights terms. Thus, in May 2011, we decided to use the occasion to launch the Connect Your Rights: Internet Rights are Human Rights campaign right in the heart of the HRC, seeking a new critical analysis of how international human rights standards applied in the context of the Internet.

CHAPTER 5

ACCOUNTABILITY IN THE UNITED NATIONS HUMAN RIGHTS COUNCIL

1. INTRODUCTION

How did the concept of human rights online formally emerge within the United Nations Human Rights Council? This chapter outlines how advocacy for freedom of expression and the Internet, by civil society groups and governments alike, helped to bring the Internet into the mainstream of the international human rights system. Through a series of careful, well-planned steps, new standards began to emerge that would crystallise the definition of an Internet-related human rights violation, culminating in the simple premise that the same human rights we have offline also apply online.

2. MAKING THE CONCEPTUAL LINK: FREEDOM OF EXPRESSION AND THE INTERNET

Although I had followed the crowds and events in Tahrir Square from afar, nothing had prepared me for the sound of their voices. I was in Geneva, participating in a panel organised by Freedom House, one of the few Internet-focussed NGOs active in the UN Human Rights Council (HRC). There I was introduced to a co-speaker, Rasha Abdullah, an Egyptian legal academic from the American University in Cairo. Her cell phone happened to ring as we were introduced, and the air between us was suddenly filled with voices chanting 'Ya ahalina endamo lina' (Friends and family, come join us).[1] As I reacted with surprise, Rasha beamed, explaining

[1] R. ABDULLA, 'The Revolution *Will* be Tweeted' *The Cairo Review of Global Affairs*, 3 (2011), 41–9, 48, available at <https://www.thecairoreview.com/essays/the-revolution-will-be-tweeted/> accessed 29.06.2020.

that it was a recording, from a few weeks earlier, of those marching to Tahrir Square; thousands of people calling in unison for others to join them. Those voices were so incredibly powerful that I can still hear them whenever I think of her.

My APC colleagues and I were in Geneva planning the Connect Your Rights campaign launch at a side event. We had invited Manal Hassan, co-founder, with Alaa Abd El-Fattah, of the award-winning Egyptian blog Manaala, because we felt that evidence of what had happened in Egypt ought to come from those who were there. We also brought speakers from other countries, each of whom could attest to the global trend of interference with freedom of expression and freedom of association on the Internet: Shahzad Ahmad, founder of the Pakistani group Bytes For All; Marina Maria, from Sexuality Policy Watch in Brazil; and Desiree Milosevic from Afilias. Johan Hallenborg, from the Swedish government's foreign ministry, and APC's executive director, Anriette Esterhuysen, co-chaired the event.

The event was, in terms of UN procedural rules, a 'side event' – literally an event on the 'side' of the 'main event', which is the regular sitting of the HRC. Despite its simple-sounding name, organising a side event was incredibly complex. Unlike an open Internet community meeting, this was no public or 'town hall' event where anyone could just turn up. Even as a seasoned lawyer, I found the rules bewildering. Because it physically took place at the UN's offices, it was subject to detailed UN rules on who could host it, what could be discussed, where it could be held, who could attend, how long it could last, what could be displayed, and myriad other prescriptions.

Getting an audience was fraught because only 'accredited' people could attend: if you were not accredited, then an invitation from an already-accredited organisation or government was required. Attendees were required to wear and display their accreditation badge, and getting such a badge could take weeks, with proof of invitation and passport identification needed before entering the UN buildings. All of these rules meant that there were only a small pool of people who might come. This pool of potential attendees was made even smaller by the fact that there would be other side events on at the same time, and all would be in the lunch hour, and so if lunch was not provided, the chances of anyone at all turning up were very slim. We were fortunate that our side event would be hosted by the Swedish government, which was very interested in Internet-related human rights discussions, and was providing funding to APC and other groups through

Sida, its international aid development arm.[2] My colleagues at APC were experts, and they happily guided me. We put out flyers, issued invitations, applied for accreditation badges, prepared statements, promoted the event as best we could, and hoped for a decent turn out.

In the days before the event, we convened a meeting of human rights groups based in Geneva, to share our concerns and seek their advice on our strategy. Phillippe Dam, of Human Rights Watch, agreed to host the meeting, to which we invited over two dozen groups. Only a handful turned up, making me very nervous about the upcoming side event. Most of the attendees were extremely busy with their own work, but all were interested in this new topic of the Internet, and had grave concerns about the Internet shutdown in Egypt. We briefed them on the La Rue report and related issues, and asked them to be critical: what did they think were the strengths and weaknesses in the advocacy strategy? What was happening in the HRC that we should be aware of? What might they be willing to support, and how could we support them? It turned out that our timing was good: there were no other groups working on the Internet and human rights at the HRC, so they thought that we could fill a clear advocacy gap. But we needed to be careful of the politics and take small, sustainable steps rather than try for large, 'flashy' actions that might be fleeting or lead to disagreements, resulting in serious setbacks.

We were cautioned to keep our expectations low. There were serious concerns that any attempt to change the UN's International Bill of Rights, or to create a new treaty on the Internet and human rights, would not only be doomed to failure, it would be misused in order to renegotiate other existing rights and freedoms.[3] One option was to see if governments might agree to a resolution focussed exclusively on the Internet and human rights. It would be no easy task, but a new, separate resolution would be much stronger, and could usefully aid interpretation of other human rights standards.

Given the deep conceptual challenges affecting human rights online, civil society groups were nervous, but Frank La Rue was bold and clear in his report, dealing with each of these challenges and providing overwhelming

---

2 See Association for Progressive Communications, *Annual Reports*, 2011–13.

3 D. SOUTER, 'Human Rights and the Internet: A Review of Perceptions' in *Human Rights Organisations*, Association for Progressive Communications, 2012, pp. 17–18, 37–38 <https://www.apc.org/en/pubs/human-rights-and-internet-review-perceptions-human> accessed 03.03.2021.

evidence of the global trend of Internet interferences. La Rue seemed to understand the concept that the Internet was a new place, not simply a tool, likening it to a '*plaza publica*' or 'public place' that did not belong to anyone, and where governments had duties to respect, protect and promote human rights. Critically, La Rue went further, linking freedom of expression as an 'enabler' of other rights, like economic, social and cultural rights. The Internet was, he said, acting as a catalyst for people to exercise their right to freedom of opinion and expression, and facilitating the realisation of other human rights. The Internet was the tool *and* the garden.

To address the concept of how an interference with the Internet could be a human rights violation, La Rue helpfully separated discussion of Internet access into two dimensions: access to online content (which should only be limited in the very few cases already permitted under international human rights law), and access to infrastructure (the availability of necessary information communication technologies, such as cables, modems, computers and software).[4]

On access to content, La Rue said that Article 19 of the UDHR, and the ICCPR, provides everyone with the right to express him or herself *through any media*, which includes future technological developments through which individuals can exercise their right to freedom of expression, such as the Internet. The international human rights legal framework, he said, was equally applicable to new communication technologies, including the Internet.[5] In effect, the Internet was free, open, machine-readable and human-readable. On access to infrastructure, La Rue said that, given the Internet's importance, states had duties to enable access, and should prioritise the development of universal Internet access.

On the questions of harms and remedies, La Rue highlighted the global trends in new human rights violations, such as criminalisation of online expression, blocking, controlling and manipulating Internet content, interference with privacy and data protection, and restrictions on Internet access, including Internet shutdowns. Such actions were, La Rue said, clear human rights violations that caused harm that warranted remedies. Specifically addressing the challenge of remedies, La Rue emphasised the need for effective remedies, including rights of appeal.[6] In addition, he noted that the Internet has created more avenues for the

---

4 F. LA RUE, United Nations Human Rights Council, 'Report of the Special Rapporteur on the Promotion and Protection of the Right to Freedom of Opinion and Expression' (A/HRC/17/27) 26.04.2011, para. 3.

5 ibid., para. 21.

6 ibid., para. 47.

use of traditional remedies, including the right of reply, the publishing of corrections, and the issuance of public apologies.[7]

With these conceptual links made, it followed that any restrictions on online freedom of expression by governments must also be exceptional, narrowly prescribed by law, and for a lawful purpose both necessary and proportionate.

La Rue's dual approach to Internet access and the idea of the Internet as a public place helped with the conceptual challenge of who ought to be accountable. Access to content engaged clear obligations of governments to respect, protect and promote human rights. Access to infrastructure, La Rue said, was necessary to prevent the creation of a 'digital divide', and to ensure that the benefits of the Internet were available to all.[8] Given that some states were still struggling with 'basic commodities such as electricity', La Rue shied away from saying that governments must provide Internet access immediately. Instead, he recommended developing policies with all stakeholders, including the private sector, 'to make the Internet widely available, accessible, and affordable to all'.[9] La Rue was effectively signalling that a multi-stakeholder approach was the way to improve access to infrastructure.

La Rue also highlighted women's human rights, and emphasised that their rights to freedom of expression and freedom of association must be respected and protected. Focusing on harm, he concluded that all forms of gender-based violence (including domestic violence, sexual violence and harassment) in both public and private spheres were forms of discrimination, and violations of women's human rights which governments must take steps to prevent.[10] This meant ensuring that laws, policies and practices did not permit or create new forms of violence against women, such as cyberstalking, digital surveillance, data monitoring and other interferences with women's rights.

La Rue's analysis went further, by suggesting ways to engage with private sector Internet providers about their human rights responsibilities. For example, he said that they should resist and refuse attempts by states to interfere with the rights of Internet users if such attempts did not comply with due process of law or agreed international norms, and ensure that any

---

7 ibid., para. 27.

8 ibid., paras. 60–62.

9 ibid., para. 66, pp. 16–7.

10 UN Committee on the Elimination of Discrimination Against Women (CEDAW), *CEDAW General Recommendation No. 19: Violence against Women* (11th session, 1992).

self-regulation of content does not infringe on the rights of users to free expression.

The HRC considered the La Rue report in a three-hour interactive dialogue that was well attended by Member States. Dozens of countries wanted to make comments and ask questions; sitting in the back of the famous Council room, the atmosphere was attentive and engaged. At the end of the HRC session, the Swedish representatives rallied support for the principle of human rights online, negotiating a cross-regional statement, presented by foreign minister Carl Bildt on behalf of more than 50 countries – up from nine the previous year.[11]

Our side event took place immediately after the interactive dialogue, and the response was incredible. Interest soared, and at one point there was standing room only. Frank La Rue attended, and our speakers were able to share their experiences. There were key focuses on the Internet shutdowns in Egypt and Pakistan, and the filtering of access to online sexual and reproductive health information in Brazil.

La Rue's report and the related side event generated a desire for more discussion about the Internet and human rights. Follow-up would be essential and the idea settled upon was that the annual resolution on freedom of expression, to be sponsored by Sweden the following September, should suggest a follow-up action, an Expert Panel, to keep the topic under discussion.

La Rue's work provided the much-needed breakthrough for those working on the conceptual challenges of the Internet as a new place, the definition of a human right violation, and the roles and responsibilities of various stakeholders in relation to Internet access. The Connect Your Rights campaign had taken important steps, but we were under no illusion: much more was needed to secure a strong connection between human rights offline and online.

3. THE EXPERT PANEL ON FREEDOM OF EXPRESSION AND THE INTERNET

The HRC uses Expert Panels for a variety of reasons: to examine particular situations affecting human rights, such as those in Sri Lanka or Syria, or

11 Office of the High Commissioner For Human Rights, 'Concept Note: Panel Discussion on Freedom of Expression on the Internet', Geneva 2012, p. 3. The concept paper is available at <https://www.apc.org/en/news/human-rights-council-panel-freedom-expression-and-internet> accessed 29.06.2020.

topical issues, such as freedom of association. The procedural rules for these panels are informal; they usually involve a three-hour debate on a pre-defined topic introduced by four or five experts who assist HRC discussions. Panels are 'safe' ways to explore a topic because there is no automatic follow-up: if the discussion does not go well, it does not matter too much. This strength is also a major drawback, however, since panels may be criticised for being too weak (discussion may be too diplomatic, or not diplomatic enough), being a 'talkfest', or may simply be disrupted by filibustering. A panel on freedom of expression and the Internet was not without risks, but also represented a unique opportunity to gauge the state of affairs in the HRC and identify conceptual sticking points or areas of consensus. It would also be the first opportunity for the HRC to have a wide-ranging discussion focussed solely on the Internet and human rights, and for all Member States and accredited NGOs to participate.

By the end of 2011, email was celebrating its fortieth birthday. Almost half of the world's email users were in Asia (49 per cent), with 22 per cent in Europe, 14 per cent in North America, and the rest of the world accounting for the remaining 15 per cent.[12] The number of Internet users climbed to 2.4 billion. There were 300 million new websites since 2010, bringing the total to 500 million. By the end of the year Facebook had reached 800 million users – some suggested that it might even reach a billion – and, in December, Twitter reached 200 million users. Hotmail was the most popular email account, with Microsoft Outlook a close second.[13] In short, the Internet was continuing its rapid evolutionary growth, and we were determined that human rights needed to evolve with it.

In September 2011 the HRC agreed to hold the Expert Panel in early 2012.[14] The HRC decided 'to convene, within existing resources … a panel discussion on the promotion and protection of freedom of expression on the Internet, with a particular focus on the ways and means to improve its protection in accordance with international human rights law'.[15] The HRC

12 The Radicati Group, 'Email Statistics Report 2011–2015 – Executive Summary' <http://www.radicati.com/wp/wp-content/uploads/2011/05/Email-Statistics-Report-2011-2015-Executive-Summary.pdf> accessed 18.06.2020.

13 Royal Pingdom, 'Internet 2011 by the Numbers', 17.01.2012 <https://royal.pingdom.com/internet-2011-in-numbers/> accessed 18.06.2020.

14 UN Human Rights Council Decision 18/27, adopted September 2011, <https://www.apc.org/en/news/human-rights-council-panel-freedom-expression-and-internet>.

15 ibid., p. 1.

also asked the High Commissioner for Human Rights, Navi Pillay, 'to liaise with relevant special procedures, States and other stakeholders, including relevant United Nations bodies and agencies, with a view to ensuring multi-stakeholder participation in the panel discussion'. This would be no side event: a multi-stakeholder panel on the Internet and human rights would be a main event in the HRC. This would also be a chance to make a crucial connection between Internet activists and human rights defenders and – another first for the international human rights system – to discuss whether human rights, in their full scope and capacity, applied to the Internet.[16]

Drawing on the Internet model for developing standards, the Expert Panel on freedom of expression and the Internet had multi-stakeholder representation. Participants were from civil society (Anriette Esterhuysen, from the APC), the technical community (Carlos Alfonso, from Instituto Nupef in Brazil), and the private sector (William Echikson, from Google), and national human rights institutions were represented by Hesti Armiwulan from the Indonesian human rights commission. Riz Khan, a senior journalist at Al Jazeera, moderated and Navi Pillay, the High Commissioner for Human Rights, made the opening statement.[17]

The Council meeting room was noisy as the panellists took their seats – full of bustle as people arrived, passed papers to one another and slowly took their seats. But as Pillay began speaking with the calm, authoritative and measured tone of a former South African constitutional court judge, the room fell quiet. Her message was clear: 'The Internet has transformed human rights movements' and 'States can no longer exercise control based on the notion of a monopoly over information.'[18] Observing the backlash that this had caused, Pillay expressed concern about tactics of blocking Internet content, including just-in-time DDoS attacks. She suggested that these actions were not merely technical in nature, but also raised

---

16 Background papers relating to the Expert Panel, as well as the HRC agenda, are available at <https://www.ohchr.org/EN/HRBodies/HRC/RegularSessions/Session19/Pages/19RegularSession.aspx> accessed 29.06.2020.

17 For more biographical information, see <https://www.ohchr.org/EN/AboutUs/Pages/NaviPillay.aspx>.

18 N. PILLAY, Opening Remarks, 'Expert Panel on Freedom of Expression and the Internet', Human Rights Council, 29.02.2012. The full video recording of the Panel is available on the UN Web TV website, along with all oral statements, at <http://webtv.un.org/search/panel-on-right-to-freedom-of-expression-19th-regular-session-human-rights-council-part-1/5252873406001/?term=2012&lan=English&cat=Meetings%2FEvents&sort=date&page=99> accessed 16.06.2020.

important policy questions. After a few brief introductory remarks by Frank La Rue, the floor opened for discussion. Sitting at the back of the room, we looked out over the scene and held our breaths.

The response was an extraordinary, if slightly surreal, spectacle: dozens of diplomats immediately began waving their flags vigorously, vying for the attention of the chair in order to secure a place in line for speaking rights; some even leapt to their feet. There was a surge of energy in the room, but ultimately there was only time for comments from about 25 governments and a handful of NGOs.

Several themes quickly emerged. Many countries affirmed their view that freedom of expression applied to the Internet, observing that the same human rights we have offline should apply online. There appeared to be consensus that existing human rights standards, including reasonable and lawful limitations on freedom of expression, should be applied to the exercise of such freedom online. The Council of Europe proposed intergovernmental cooperation, and India suggested global Internet governance principles. There were many references to the effect of the Internet on democratic engagement and mobilisation, and concerns about Internet shutdowns, including those in the Middle East and North Africa, most specifically Egypt. The private sector was recognised as an important stakeholder, and was called on to uphold human rights under the UN principles developed by Professor John Ruggie for business and human rights (for example, by not exporting surveillance technologies or engaging in national tenders for filtering and blocking technologies).[19]

Overall, discussion was measured, balanced, and constructive. There were no significant fissures; the issues were generally as expected, and in line with the evidence in the La Rue report. Significantly, there were no conceptual debates about whether the Internet was a tool or a space, or whether an interference with the Internet could be a human rights violation. There were no calls to add new human rights, although the efforts to create declarations of Internet rights and principles were acknowledged. Crucially, the question of who was in control of the Internet was not raised. Instead, discussion about accountability for human rights on the Internet focussed squarely on the role of governments to respect and protect human rights, and ensure that any limitations were necessary, proportionate and

---

[19] Oral statement by the Netherlands at 'Expert Panel on Freedom of Expression and the Internet', Human Rights Council, 29.02.2012. See weblink in n. 18 above.

prescribed by law. It was a good outcome, and the chair declared the discussion 'a success'.[20] The next step would be for the HRC to consider the summary report at its next meeting and decide what, if any, further actions to take.[21]

4. THE UNIVERSAL PERIODIC REVIEW

During the Expert Panel discussion, it was suggested that the HRC focus on the issue of the Internet in the newly introduced Universal Periodic Review (UPR). The UPR had been established in the HRC as a political response to problems with the treaty bodies, which were criticised not only for being too slow and cumbersome, but also being unable to take a holistic view of the entire human rights situation in a given country. Human rights monitoring was divided into civil and political rights; racial discrimination; discrimination against women; economic, cultural and social rights; and the rights of children and disabled people. Many were finding the myriad of processes exhausting, and called for a fundamental rethink of how to examine all human rights in any given country, as well as how to respond to new and emerging issues. There were also criticisms of the overlapping work programmes of the Geneva- and New York-based human rights bodies.[22]

The UPR was an entirely new process designed to be shorter, more regular, more holistic, and with peer, rather than expert, review.[23] In the UPR, countries would report to, and question, each other about human rights and make recommendations for improvements, which could be either accepted or rejected. Countries would report to the HRC (assisted by a small working group of three states) through a periodic four-year cycle that included in-country consultation with civil society on progress, formal country reporting, examination by the HRC, and agreed

---

20 Concluding remarks by the vice chair, available at the weblink in n. 18 above.

21 UN Human Rights Council, 'Summary of the Human Rights Council Panel Discussion on the Promotion and Protection of Freedom of Expression on the Internet – Report of the Office of the UN High Commissioner for Human Rights', A/HRC/21/30.

22 S. PHUANGKETKEOW, *Report of the Open-ended Working Group on Review of the Work and Functioning of Human Rights Council*, United Nations General Assembly, 04.05.2011, A/HRC/WG.8/2/1. See also the working papers at <https://www.ohchr.org/EN/HRBodies/HRC/Pages/HRCReview.aspx> accessed 04.05.2021.

23 New Zealand Ministry of Foreign Affairs and Trade, *United Nations Handbook 2019–20*, Ministry of Foreign Affairs and Trade, Wellington 2019, p. 32.

recommendations for improvements and implementation.[24] The new process was very streamlined but also inherently political, since it was a peer review. The HRC would hold three formal sittings per year, each one considering the UPR reports of various countries, with civil society groups and national human rights institutions also participating.

In early 2012, as the Expert Panel took place, the HRC was also busy with the new UPR process. Though it was early days, the process seemed to be working well. My recent experiences in the New Zealand Human Rights Commission persuaded me that this new type of review was the ideal way to build on the constructive dialogue at the panel. In a 'universal' review, *any* human rights issue can be raised, including new ones such as the Internet and human rights. Here was the perfect opportunity to bring to the HRC the many diverse examples of Internet interference from around the world. The key messages of the Connect Your Rights campaign could be amplified with the help of civil society groups, experiences could be shared, and lessons learned and applied quickly to others. Doing so promptly after the Expert Panel would also enable us to amplify and reinforce the HRC's developing approach to human rights online, and hold to account those governments who participated in the HRC.

With an existing global network of civil society groups all linked to national organisations, and with expertise about the Internet, I was convinced APC was ideally placed to take the issues forward in a coordinated advocacy national regional and global strategy. Such a strategy would also enable Internet groups to build mutually beneficial relationships with the human rights groups that were still new to the Internet, and Internet groups still new to the international human rights system. In our meetings with human rights groups in 2011, there was support for such a strategy, particularly because there were no other groups focussed on the Internet in the UPR: the timing was perfect.

Having agreed on a strategy, the immediate issue was to decide which countries to focus on. The rotation of country reports and review dates had been set two years before, and some were already under way. There were a lot factors to consider: each country had a different human rights situation, and a different level of government and other stakeholder participation in the Internet Governance Forum (IGF) and the Internet Corporation for Assigned Names and Numbers (ICANN). It was necessary to decide which strategic issues to highlight (perhaps freedom of expression, Internet access, or freedom of association), who had capacity and capability and

24 ibid.

how to highlight the regional differences across the world. In the end, the four countries were those whose reviews were due shortly: India, Brazil, South Africa and Ecuador.[25]

Some reviews were more successful than others. In Brazil, for example, local groups Instituto Nupef and Sexuality Policy Watch filed a report on internet-related human rights issues, and this was considered at their country's review in May 2012, right after the Expert Panel. Brazil accepted a recommendation from Estonia to give freedom of expression more consideration when developing national cybercrime legislation, in order to ensure the protection of this fundamental right.[26] This proved useful support in March 2014, when Brazil passed the landmark Marco de Civil.

In Ecuador, local groups CIESPAL and Radialistas Apasionadas y Apasionados filed a report on issues of Internet access, highlighting the critical importance of the Internet for human rights and social and economic development.[27] However, despite subsequent government offers to work with civil society in drafting communications legislation that respected human rights, Ecuador's Organic Communications Law of June 2013 placed new limitations on anonymity and freedom of expression, and proposed dangerous new amendments to the new criminal code, which would violate the right to privacy by requiring Internet intermediaries to store data on all users.

India's Digital Empowerment Foundation filed a report focussing on the right to information and freedom of expression online, and their recommendations relating to access to information and the Internet were among those accepted by their government.[28] During the review, India noted the recommendation by Sweden to 'ensure that measures limiting freedom of expression on the internet is based on clearly defined criteria in accordance with international human rights standards'.[29]

A coalition of South African civil society groups filed a report on freedom of expression, the right to information, freedom from censorship,

---

25 For an overview, see 'Universal Periodic Review' <https://www.apc.org/en/project/universal-periodic-review> accessed 30.06.2020.

26 UN Human Rights Council, 'Report of the Working Group on the Universal Periodic Review: Brazil', A/HRC/21/11, para. 119, p. 22.

27 UN Human Rights Council, 'Report of the Working Group on the Universal Periodic Review: Ecuador', A/HRC/21/4.

28 UN Human Rights Council, 'Report of the Working Group on the Universal Periodic Review: India', A/HRC/WG.6/13/L.8, para. 138, pp. 14–24.

29 UN Human Rights Council, 'Report of the Working Group on the Universal Periodic Review: India', A/HRC/WG.6/13/L.8, para. 75, p. 9, and see also recommendation 126 at para. 138, p. 22.

freedom of the press, the right to privacy, and the importance of affordable access to the Internet.[30] This coalition included many mainstream human rights groups, such as the Centre for Applied Legal Studies, Gender Links, the Highway Africa Chair of Media and Information Society, Open Democracy Advice Centre, Right2Know, the Southern African NGO Network (SANGONeT), Section27, and the Socio-Economic Rights Institute of South Africa.[31]

The UPR also provided avenues to help organisations already engaged in the review process by adding Internet issues. Internet rights groups made connections with the Human Rights Institute of South Africa (HURISA), for example, which led a coalition participating in other issues in the South African review. In turn, HURISA reached out to the South African Human Rights Commission, which was dealing with a number of high-profile cases of abusive speech online. In 2013, the APC reported that the Commission announced its first successful facilitation of a complaint involving the Internet, with the resolution 'including a public apology and withdrawal of all hurtful racial statements posted on social media by a young journalist.'[32] In 2012, the International Partnership Group for Azerbaijan also made a submission to the Azerbaijani review, raising concerns about the perilous situation there, including for women's human rights defenders such as Khadija Ismayilova.[33]

The UPR, over time, proved to be an extremely useful way to advocate for respect and protection of human rights online, but all of that was still a long way off. In the meantime, significant scepticism remained that anything sensible could come from involving governments in questions about the Internet. Such scepticism was well placed, especially given the different regulatory approaches of various governments. A good understanding of human rights and the Internet was developing in the HRC: there were no apparent conceptual sticking points and many areas of apparent consensus. But the Expert Panel had no clear outcomes and would be viewed as ineffectual unless there was more. An HRC resolution on human rights and the Internet was the logical next step.

---

30 Centre for Applied Legal Studies and others 'Joint Submission to the Universal Periodic Review of the Republic of South Africa', South Africa, 28 November 2011.

31 ibid.

32 Association for Progressive Communications, 'Universal Periodic Review: South Africa', <https://www.apc.org/en/project/universal-periodic-review> accessed 05.03.2021.

33 The Free Library, 'The International Partnership Group urged the United Nations to Put Pressure on Azerbaijan', <https://www.thefreelibrary.com/The+International+Partnership+Group+urged+the+United+Nations+to+Put ... -a0416860072> accessed 05.03.2021.

5. THE RESOLUTION ON HUMAN RIGHTS AND THE INTERNET

Although not binding or enforceable, a UN resolution carries significant weight, being a formal expression of opinion that can provide policy recommendations for Member States to follow.[34] For example, UN resolutions established the Internet Governance Forum and led to the Beijing Platform for Action. The process of negotiating resolutions can be very technical, taking many days, weeks, months, or even years to find drafting language on which all parties can agree. To speed this process up for the Internet and human rights, some looked to communications rights and the new charters of Internet rights and principles for possible guidance.

However, many human rights groups did not favour the idea of a resolution on 'Internet rights' or the creation of new standards for the Internet alone.[35] On the contrary, they felt that the international regime was already able to address the impact of the Internet, and that 'there is no case for or merit in amending the international instruments'.[36] Research showed that there was a 'paradigm gap' between the perceptions of human rights groups, who felt that the effects of the Internet were often overstated by fervent Internet rights activists, and the perceptions of Internet rights organisations, who felt that their concerns were not being taken seriously enough.[37]

Negotiation of UN resolutions takes place through a mix of open and closed meetings. Following the Expert Panel, the Swedish representatives decided to develop a draft resolution, and commenced consultation meetings in the lead-up to the following HRC session. The open consultation meeting in Geneva was attended by governments and NGOs, and focussed on suggestions for the draft text including: calling on states to cooperate on global policymaking and Internet governance; a reference to all human rights rather than only freedom of expression; mentioning some specific rights, such as privacy and freedom of association; referring to the importance of an open Internet or to Internet access; or of the need to balance freedom of expression with limitations, such as against incitement to racial hatred.[38]

---

34 United Nations DAG repository <http://ask.un.org/faq/14484> accessed 05.03.2021.

35 D. SOUTER, above n. 3, pp. 17–18, 37–38.

36 ibid., p. 20.

37 ibid., p. 15.

38 Email notes of the open consultation provided to the author by a participant in June 2012.

A few amendments were made (such as inclusion of a reference to an open Internet, which was important for the technical community), and the draft text was tabled by Sweden, along with more than 80 co-sponsors, for the HRC's to consider. On 5 July 2012, the HRC adopted the draft by consensus, meaning that no country opposed the resolution.[39] The resolution stated that the HRC:[40]

1. *Affirms* that the same rights that people have offline must also be protected online, in particular freedom of expression, which is applicable regardless of frontiers and through any media of one's choice, in accordance with articles 19 of the Universal Declaration of Human Rights and the International Covenant on Civil and Political Rights;
2. *Recognizes* the global and open nature of the Internet as a driving force in accelerating progress towards development in its various forms;
3. *Calls upon* all States to promote and facilitate access to the Internet and international cooperation aimed at the development of media and information and communications facilities in all countries;
4. *Encourages* special procedures to take these issues into account within their existing mandates, as applicable;
5. *Decides* to continue its consideration of the promotion, protection and enjoyment of human rights, including the right to freedom of expression, on the Internet and in other technologies, as well as of how the Internet can be an important tool for development and for exercising human rights, in accordance with its programme of work.

The adoption of the resolution by consensus, and such an overwhelming one, was surprising. For example, there were fears that some countries

---

39 The full list of co-sponsors is: Algeria*, Argentina*, Australia*, Austria, Azerbaijan*, Belgium, Bolivia (Plurinational State of)*, Bosnia and Herzegovina*, Brazil*, Bulgaria*, Canada*, Chile, Costa Rica, Côte d'Ivoire*, Croatia*, Cyprus*, Czech Republic, Denmark*, Djibouti, Egypt*, Estonia*, Finland*, France*, Georgia*, Germany*, Greece*, Guatemala, Honduras*, Hungary, Iceland*, India, Indonesia, Ireland*, Italy, Latvia*, Libya, Liechtenstein*, Lithuania*, Luxembourg*, Maldives, Malta*, Mauritania, Mexico, Monaco*, Montenegro*, Morocco*, Netherlands*, Nigeria, Norway, Palestine*, Peru, Poland, Portugal*, Qatar, Republic of Moldova, Republic of Korea*, Romania, Serbia*, Slovakia*, Slovenia*, Somalia*, Spain, Sweden*, the former Yugoslav Republic of Macedonia*, Timor-Leste*, Tunisia*, Turkey*, Ukraine*, United Kingdom of Great Britain and Northern Ireland*, United States of America, Uruguay [* denotes Non-Member State of the HRC].

40 UN Human Rights Council, resolution on 'The Promotion, Protection and Enjoyment of Human Rights on the Internet' A/HRC/RES/20/8, adopted by the HRC (A/HRC/20/2, (Chapter 1)), 16.07.2012.

might oppose the resolution or formally abstain, rendering it political, and significantly weakening its force. The number of countries co-sponsoring was also surprising since, just two years earlier, only 20 countries supported the annual resolution on freedom of expression. I was a little disappointed that the resolution did not go further: there were no references, for example, to women's human rights, or to the rights to privacy and freedom of association. After all, it was 2012: was the resolution not just a simple, self-evident statement of the rather obvious? In addition, there was a significant gap, namely, the human rights duties of social media platforms. Some criticism was fair, but, as we have seen, the case for human rights online had not been straightforward.

Ultimately, the resolution was historic: the first clear statement from the HRC that human rights applied online.[41] The resolution was a solid step forward and Carl Bildt, the Swedish foreign minister, heralded it as a 'victory for the Internet'.[42]

6. CONNECTING HUMAN RIGHTS AND INTERNET GOVERNANCE

The resolution came as a surprise to many outside the HRC. Few of those involved in Internet governance were following HRC events, mainly because it was not an open, multi-stakeholder forum of the kind they were used to, but also because there was an awful lot going on in Internet governance in 2012. A significant exception was the Internet Society, which had participated in discussions of both the Expert Panel and the draft HRC resolution, mainly being based in Geneva and already accredited to the UN. Their engagement was cautious – they feared that governments might attempt to use discussions in the HRC to assert control over the Internet, rather than to respect its existing multi-stakeholder nature, and the processes that made it function so well – but they were happy with the resolution.[43]

---

41 M. KOTHARI, 'The Sameness of Human Rights Online and Offline' in M. SUSI (ed.) *Human Rights, Digital Society and the Law: A Research Companion*, Routledge, London 2019.

42 C. BILDT, 'A Victory for the Internet,' Op-ed., *New York Times*, (New York, 5 July 2012) <https://www.nytimes.com/2012/07/06/opinion/carl-bildt-a-victory-for-the-internet.html?_r=1> accessed 18.06.2020.

43 Personal communication with the author, June 2012.

By 2012, the IGF had grown enormously, sparking many national and even regional initiatives.[44] The seventh global IGF, planned for November in Baku, was preceded by more than a dozen national and regional Internet governance conferences, and many people were deeply engaged in preparations. In 2010, the sixth IGF was held in Nairobi, sub-Saharan Africa's first time hosting the event, and the largest event so far. There, the governments of India, Brazil and South Africa put forward proposals for establishing a new 'Internet oversight' body within the UN system, prompting vigorous debate on a controversial challenge to the technical community's operation of the Internet.

As preparations began for Baku, these discussions about Internet governance, inevitably, ground to a stalemate amid divergent views and political tensions. There were lengthy discussions on definitions (What was the Internet? What was regulation? What were human rights?) and the best, or most appropriate forms of regulation or regulatory approaches. In the end, much of the preparation for the IGF was focussed on inching towards a consensus that, instead of adopting the India proposal, a new UN working group should be established to consider the meaning of 'enhanced cooperation' among various stakeholders.[45]

Despite this controversy, barely a quarter of the more than 80 governments supporting the HRC resolution turned up to the Baku IGF. The absence of governments was evidence that the political importance of the IGF was waning, and some stakeholders had concerns that there might be more attempts to exert control over the Internet in some other way. The plethora of multi-stakeholder initiatives promoting Internet rights and principles (discussed in Chapter 4) was also causing problems, and raising more questions than answers: for instance, what was the meaning of these various principles? How and by whom would they be enforced? And how they might relate to existing global agreements and standards? The Internet Rights and Principles Dynamic Coalition proposed a step forward by suggesting that the IGF should provide a space for establishing whether there was consensus on these various declarations of rights and principles, but this did not gain support.

---

44 In 2012, there were 9 regional, 16 national and 2 youth Internet governance initiatives: see <https://www.intgovforum.org/cms/component/content/article/114-preparatory-process/1281-igf-initiatives-2012> accessed 02.12.2020.

45 UN General Assembly Resolution, 'Information and Communications Technologies for Development' (resolution /67/195), which invited the chair of the Commission on Science and Technology for Development to 'establish a working group on enhanced cooperation', 23.01.2013, para. 20.

The proximity of the HRC resolution to the IGF did have some positive effects. Discussion about human rights featured prominently, with technical, private sector and civil society participants using human rights language to frame many of their interventions. Of the 127 workshops, main sessions, dynamic coalitions, side sessions, open fora, and sessions on capacity building, 82 addressed some aspect of human rights on the Internet.[46] Recurrent themes included privacy, freedom of expression, access to information, data rights, cybersecurity, and Internet intermediary liability; some new human rights issues also emerged, such as the right to anonymity.[47]

One very memorable moment brought home to me the power of the multi-stakeholder environment. It occurred as European Commissioner Neelie Kroes addressed a workshop. Kroes mentioned the Azerbaijani journalist Eynulla Fatullayev, who had recently won the UNESCO World Press Freedom Prize.[48] When someone pointed out that he was in the room, she immediately went over to greet him, giving him a big hug. For me, this was exactly the sort of serendipity that could only occur at an open, inclusive event where many different stakeholders were present. It was in stark contrast to the carefully controlled procedural rules and choreographed side events in the halls of the UN buildings in Geneva, and left me wondering whether it would really be possible to create deeper links between the IGF and the HRC, as well as between human rights online and offline.

One particular concern was how to advance women's rights at the IGF. While gender and women's empowerment were, for the first time, included as main session topics at the IGF in Baku, only one workshop dealt with gender issues specifically. Speakers in the main sessions and workshops were mostly male.[49] This weak approach to women's human rights was highlighted, just before the IGF, by an attack on one of our network's human rights defenders.

---

46 Based on textual keyword analysis of transcripts of workshops and main sessions.

47 Association for Progressive Communications, 'IGF 2012: the Good, the Bad and the Ugly', 14.02.2013 <https://www.apc.org/en/pubs/igf-2012-good-bad-and-ugly> accessed 05.03.2021.

48 United Nations, 'Azerbaijani Journalist Selected for Annual UN Press Freedom Award', press release, 17.04.2012 <https://news.un.org/en/story/2012/04/408842-azerbaijani-journalist-selected-annual-un-press-freedom-award> accessed 18.06.2020.

49 F. FASCENDINI, 'Gender report card at the IGF 2012', Association for Progressive Communications, 31 October 2012 <https://www.apc.org/en/news/gender-inclusion-igf-gender-report-card> accessed 05.03.2021.

On 9 October 2012, a young Pakistani schoolgirl and her two friends were travelling home by bus after taking a school exam. Just 15 years old, Malala Yousafzai was already well known for her blog on life in the Swat region, and her advocacy for girls' right to education.[50] As the girls travelled home, a gunman entered the bus, shot Malala and fled the scene. The Taliban later claimed responsibility for the assassination attempt, made in retaliation for her activism. There was global condemnation of the cowardly attack, as Malala was hit in the head with a bullet and critically injured.[51] Her subsequent recovery and brave ongoing activism resulted in her being a co-recipient, in 2014, of the Nobel Peace Prize, with Kailash Satyarthi of India.[52]

Malala had been a target of online harassment long before the assassination attempt. She started receiving death threats soon after her identity was made public as the author of the BBC's 'Diary of a Pakistani schoolgirl', in which she denounced the atrocities that took place during Taliban rule, under the pen name Gul Makai.[53] Several Facebook pages dedicated to condemning her work had been set up[54] and, in March 2012, Tehrik-e-Taliban Pakistan announced that she and another social worker named Shad Begum were on the militants' hit list.[55]

In the months before the attempt on her life, Malala attended digital rights training workshops in Swat and Peshawar run by the Digital Rights Foundation, an APC member. Nighat Dad, a lawyer and prominent member of APC's women's rights network, founded the Digital Rights Foundation in Pakistan in 2012 to offer support and training on digital rights, especially for women and girls.[56] Malala had become a strong advocate for communication rights, and an active participant in APC's

---

50 BBC News, 'Malala Yousafzai: Portrait of the Girl Blogger', 12.10.2012 <https://www.bbc.com/news/magazine-19899540> accessed 07.07.2020.

51 For more information about Malala and her story, see The Malala Foundation <https://www.malala.org/> accessed 07.07.2020.

52 The Norwegian Nobel Prize Committee, 'The Nobel Peace Prize for 2014' <https://www.nobelprize.org/prizes/peace/2014/press-release/> accessed 07.07.2020.

53 BBC News, 'Diary of a Pakistani schoolgirl', 19.01.2009 <http://news.bbc.co.uk/2/hi/south_asia/7834402.stm> accessed 07.07.2020.

54 S. KHAN, 'Taking a Stand against Cyberbullying of Women in Pakistan', Global Citizen 22.01.2016 <https://global-citizen.com/cyber-bullying-women-pakistan-nighat-dad/> accessed 07.07.2020.

55 Association for Progressive Communications, 'Attack on Pakistani Youth will not Shake Women's Rights Activists', 31.10.2012 <https://www.apc.org/en/news/attack-pakistani-youth-activist-will-not-shake-wom> accessed 07.07.2020.

56 For more information about the Digital Rights Foundation, see <https://digitalrightsfoundation.pk/> accessed 07.07.2020.

'Take Back the Tech!' campaign in Pakistan.[57] Like others, we condemned the shooting. Coming so soon after the HRC resolution, the incident hardened our resolve to push for human rights online and offline, and to raise these issues in the IGF and beyond. We did not yet know it, but the campaign to connect human rights and the Internet in the digital age laid vital groundwork for responding to shocking news about mass surveillance of Internet traffic that would break in June 2013.

57 Above, n. 55.

PART II

NEW CHALLENGES IN THE DIGITAL ERA

CHAPTER 6
HUMAN RIGHTS IN THE DIGITAL AGE

1. INTRODUCTION

By early 2013, visibility of the Internet and human rights was increasing in the HRC and related UN human rights processes. Activists were developing tools to protect emerging new rights (such as rights to encryption and anonymity),[1] and calling for strengthened rights for LGBTQI+ people through initiatives such as the feminist principles for the Internet.[2] In following up his earlier work, Frank La Rue was investigating the use of technologies for state surveillance, and I attended the HRC in June to support the presentation of his latest report. While I was there, a story broke about mass surveillance: a story that would not only catapult human rights into the digital age, but also set the technical community on a collision course with human rights communities. This chapter outlines how these revelations about mass surveillance led to the international human rights system developing, with the help of human rights and technical communities, new concepts of privacy, and new definitions of human rights violations in the digital age.

2. SURVEILLANCE AND THE RIGHT TO PRIVACY

On 6 June 2013, the *Guardian* and *Washington Post* newspapers simultaneously published a story that would shock the world. Based on documents leaked by a former United States National Security Agency contractor, Edward Snowden, the story was an exposé of a vast cell

---

1 See, e.g. D. AUERBACH, '2012 in Review: Encrypting the Web with HTTPS' Electronic Frontier Foundation, 01.01.2013 <https://www.eff.org/deeplinks/2012/12/end-year-blog-post-2012-https-rise> accessed 14.12.2020.

2 Association for Progressive Communications, 'The Feminist Principles of the Internet', v.1, 2014, available at <www.feministinternet.org> accessed 15.07.2020.

phone surveillance system operated by the government of the United States of America.[3] Documents showed 'for the first time' that, under the Obama administration, the communication records of millions of US citizens were being collected 'indiscriminately and in bulk – regardless of whether they are suspected of any wrongdoing'.[4] An order by the Foreign Intelligence Surveillance Court (a court closed to the public) had granted unlimited authority for the FBI to collect, for three months, not only the contents of telephone communications, but all related call records or 'telephony metadata' from within the US, and between the US and overseas.[5] The revelations showed how vulnerable the average Internet user's communications were to interception. The intelligence agencies' surveillance strategy was simple: 'collect it all'.[6]

The revelations became a 'sputnik moment' for both mainstream human rights groups and the wider global public alike: suddenly the danger of government Internet interference was all too clear, and right above them. As we saw in Chapter 2, long before Greenwald broke his shocking story, human rights defenders and Internet activists around the world were well aware of covert telephony or Internet surveillance by law enforcement and other state agencies. The possibility of this type of surveillance taking place was predicted as early as 2000[7] but, even for seasoned Internet activists, the scale of this surveillance was unprecedented. Previously, Internet shutdowns in Egypt had stirred debate about whether Internet interferences were human rights violations in and of themselves. This time, the answers were more readily available, resulting in both near-universal condemnation of the programme *and* agreement that such surveillance was a human rights violation.

I say 'near-universal' because there were deep conceptual differences between the 'Five Eyes' alliance (the US, UK, Canada, Australia and New Zealand) and others about the relationship between technology,

---

3 G. GREENWALD, 'NSA Collecting Phone Records of Millions of Verizon Customers Daily', *The Guardian*, 06.06.2013 <https://www.theguardian.com/world/2013/jun/06/nsa-phone-records-verizon-court-order> accessed 09.07.2020.

4 ibid.

5 ibid.

6 A. COMNINOS and G. SENEQUE, 'Cyber Security, Civil Society and Vulnerability in an Age of Communications Surveillance' in *Global Information Society Watch 2014: Communications Surveillance in the Digital Age*, Association for Progressive Communications and Hivos, 2014, pp. 32–40, at p. 35–8 <https://www.giswatch.org/2014-communications-surveillance-digital-age> accessed 05.03.2021.

7 See, e.g. S. WRIGHT, 'Political Control and the Internet' in S. HICK, E. F. HALPIN and E. HOSKINS (eds.), *Human Rights and the Internet*, Macmillan Press, London 2000, pp. 200–09, at pp. 204–09.

the right to privacy and state surveillance. As we saw in Chapter 2, governments, for example in Europe, both before and after World War II, used technology to interfere with human rights and create oppressive surveillance states. As these regimes fell, and the new era of international human rights rose, many of the new governments and their citizens came to consider that technological surveillance must be vigorously restrained, with many countries developing strong national and constitutional privacy protections.

In stark contrast, intelligence agencies in the 'Five Eyes' alliance had used technology to defend themselves from attack in World War II, by developing a network for spying and intelligence-gathering on German and other forces. Having won that war, these agencies considered their use of surveillance technology to be a legitimate means of self-defence that should not only be permitted, but be as unrestrained as possible, and they developed a secret and extensive intelligence-sharing agreement known as SIGINT.[8]

The hard truth, writ large by the *Guardian* and *Washington Post* stories, was that these deep divisions still existed. Many governments were caught off guard by the legal justification for and extent of the mass surveillance programme Greenwald revealed.

3. RESPONDING TO THE CONCEPTUAL CHALLENGES

I happened to be at the UN in Geneva when the news broke. As we hurried to grasp the enormity of what had happened, my colleagues and I also knew that we had to help others to understand the technology, and work out how best to answer the impending tidal wave of questions about human rights and the Internet. Many human rights organisations were, understandably, struggling and, having been deeply involved in these issues for just a few years myself, I knew how important it was to have trusted people who could mentor, explain, and help organisations reach their own conclusions and develop their own views. In the midst of the media storm, organisations asked hard questions about technology and human rights, many echoing

[8] For a detailed history, see Privacy International, 'Eyes Wide Open' (Special Report) 26.11.2013 <https://privacyinternational.org/report/1126/eyes-wide-open> accessed 05.03.2021; and, for useful background reading, see N. HAGER, *Secret Power*, Craig Potton Publishing, Nelson (New Zealand) 1996.

the conceptual challenges outlined in Chapter 3 above. Was this a human rights violation, namely, with a right, rights-holder and duty-bearer, an interference that caused harm, and a remedy?

Several rights were immediately identified including the rights to freedom of expression and privacy. Article 17 of the ICCPR protects the right to privacy, broadly providing that 'no one shall be subjected to arbitrary interference with his privacy, family, home or correspondence'.[9] But there were many questions in this case.

Legal scholars, for example, argued over whether the actions fell within the scope of the right to privacy: were emails 'correspondence'? If so, was there a right to privacy in emails or other Internet communications? Could there be expectations of privacy when sharing information over an open network like the Internet? More complex was the issue of whether metadata (data about a communication *itself* rather than its content, for example the time an email was sent, where it was sent to and from, and any related IP address information) was 'correspondence' or other personal information falling within the scope of the protected right. If not, there would be no protection and, therefore, no human rights violation. On the other hand, metadata might fall within the right to privacy because, in some cases, it could provide *more* information about a person than the content of a communication itself, such as by indicating where and when a person was at a specific location and the type of device they were using.

If there were relevant rights and rights-holders (those individuals whose records were collected), who were the duty-bearers? The United States government argued that its obligations to uphold human rights standards only applied to its citizens within the United States, not to non-US citizens outside its physical territories. Accordingly, it was not a duty-bearer to non-US citizens, and could not be held accountable for actions against them.[10] In relation to US citizens, the collection of data had been sanctioned by a court order making it, so the argument went, lawful and therefore not an arbitrary interference.

Finally, since the information was being gathered, not by a panopticon watching everybody, but by collection of non-personal business records

---

9 International Covenant on Civil and Political Rights, 1966, Article 17.

10 For an outline of some of the arguments, see, e.g. A. J. CERDA SILVA, 'The Myth of Global Online Surveillance Exempted from Compliance with Human Rights' in *Global Information Society Watch 2014 – Communications Surveillance in the Digital Age*, Association for Progressive Communications and Hivos, 2014, pp. 25–28, <https://www.giswatch.org/2014-communications-surveillance-digital-age> accessed 05.03.2021.

about Internet and cell phone traffic, most individuals were blithely unaware that their metadata was being collected. Where was the harm?

Unlike in the case of the Internet shutdown in Egypt, this time human rights groups were ready, with both the evidence and educational materials to respond to these arguments. The HRC had already agreed that the same human rights applied offline and online. As public shock and outrage about the surveillance grew, Internet rights groups were able to respond quickly, helping to educate the public and support legal investigations. The conceptual arguments quickly fell away, and the legal focus turned away from whether or not mass surveillance was a human rights violation. Instead, the focus shifted to the rule of law and due process: what were the legal grounds for such mass surveillance? What was the legal authority of the secret, closed courts that seemed to operate without due process? And did any accountability rest with private sector companies complying with such orders?

Frank La Rue had recently completed a report on state surveillance, and this could not have come at a better time. His report examined the new methods of communications surveillance being used by governments, such as targeted and mass surveillance, access to communications data, Internet filtering, and unjustified restrictions on online anonymity. La Rue explained how metadata can reveal sensitive information which can be easily accessed, stored, exploited and mined. He recommended that metadata be protected, and that legislation authorising surveillance be updated to be compliant with international human rights law.[11] La Rue also called out private companies for their role in generating 'a global industry focused on the exchange of surveillance technologies … often sold to countries in which there is serious risk they will be used to violate human rights, particularly those of human rights defenders, journalists and other vulnerable groups'.[12]

La Rue presented his report to the HRC the day before the revelations broke, and a follow-up public side event had already been planned to highlight his findings. The response to the side event was overwhelming, the atmosphere electric. It was an incredible privilege to be there, and be able to play a part in helping human rights defenders and Internet rights advocates work together in a new and powerful way. Groups such as Privacy International, Amnesty International, Human Rights Watch, Article 19, CIVICUS and many others reached out to Internet governance

---

11 F. LA RUE, 'Annual Report of the Special Rapporteur on Freedom of Opinion and Expression', UN Human Rights Council, 17.04.2013, A/HRC/23/40, pp. 20–23.

12 ibid., paras. 74–75, pp. 19–20.

networks for help, and many people in such networks stepped up: helping with answers, or connecting people with other groups around the world, such as the Electronic Frontier Foundation, Global Voices Advocacy, and the Centre for Technology and Society.

In just a few days, a global network grew rapidly, thanks to advocates such as Deborah Brown at Access Now, Carly Nyst at Privacy International, Anja Kovacs at the Internet Democracy Project, and many others who worked hard, collaborating to draft and issue a joint statement to the HRC, and sharing information across national and global Internet communities and networks. The statement called on the HRC to convene a special session to examine the case. It supported Frank La Rue's report, and asked the High Commissioner to investigate state practices, and the actions of the private sector.[13] It also asked the HRC to draw on the UN Guiding Principles on Business and Human Rights, developed by Professor John Ruggie, to set out the responsibilities of the private sector to protect and respect human rights, and to remedy their human rights violations.[14] This work would be critical to discussions on duty-bearers, and the responsibilities of private companies which had complied with these kinds of orders.

Members of the Internet Governance Forum (IGF) community also responded quickly. Many were worried that such a sweeping unlawful use of technology for surveillance could generate a huge backlash against the technical community, and persuade enough governments to agree to regulate the Internet, to force coercive controls on how it worked, something none of them wanted. Just as many human rights organisations were suddenly grasping the Internet and human rights online, many in the Internet community had to grasp how the international human rights system worked. The differences between how each of these systems worked were suddenly in sharp relief.

Looking back, it is still difficult to express how intense the situation was, how hard we worked and, even now, to accurately summarise the flurry of questions and answers each community had of the other. But two strong themes stand out between the human rights and Internet communities: some said that it was time to acknowledge that the open, decentralised

---

13 S. FINNEGAN and C. NYST 'US-based surveillance and data collection: New UN report provides guidance on PRISM', Association for Progressive Communications and Privacy International, 13.06.2013 <https://www.apc.org/en/news/us-based-surveillance-and-data-collection-new-un-r> accessed 16.03.2021.

14 United Nations 'Guiding Principles on Business and Human Rights: Implementing the United Nations "Protect, Respect and Remedy" Framework', 21.03.2011, A/HRC/17/31. The HRC created an expert working group on business and human rights to take forward recommendations in the report.

nature of the Internet was being exploited by unscrupulous governments; actions which the Internet community was not ready or able to stop, and which human rights were the best protection against. Others denounced the government actions but, given how unscrupulously even democratic governments were behaving in and around the Internet, thought that there was good reason to be deeply cynical about the idea that the international human rights system, run by those same governments, would be an answer to these human rights violations.

The various responses also traversed well-known weaknesses in the international human rights system. For example, several human rights groups suggested making a complaint about the mass surveillance to the UN Human Rights Committee, the treaty body monitoring the International Covenant on Civil and Political Rights. The suggestion was quite sensible from a traditional human rights perspective: the committees are designed for this kind of role. However, there was a real sense of urgency in the need for a strong legal response and this kind of complaint would take far too long to resolve: possibly years. There was no one on the committee with the expertise to handle this kind of complaint, and the process of getting such a person would inevitably become political, since the appointment would need to be made by national governments. Another suggestion was to ask the same committee to issue a new General Comment on privacy: privacy groups had been calling for a new comment for some years, and felt that the revelations could help push this request along. But the committee decides its work programme a year in advance, and had apparently already decided to focus on the right to life, so a new General Comment would not be possible for at least two years: a lifetime on the Internet.

In the end, a strategy similar to that of 2011 was developed: support an Expert Panel at the HRC to garner evidence, secure an in-depth report by the High Commissioner, bring forward a series of new resolutions, and help educate the public about their own digital security. Within weeks of the revelations, Navi Pillay, the High Commissioner for Human Rights who had so ably participated in the panel on freedom of expression and the Internet just two years before, had drawn on Frank La Rue's report to speak out against mass surveillance which threatened human rights.[15] In December 2013, Germany and Brazil, two key governments both affected and embarrassed by the revelations, sponsored a UN General

[15] N. PILLAY, 'Opening Remarks by the UN Human Rights Chief to the Side Event at the 24th Session of the Human Rights Council: How to Safeguard Privacy in the

Assembly resolution rebuking unlawful surveillance and data collection, and calling for an investigation by Pillay's office.[16] The following March, the HRC decided to convene an expert panel on the right to privacy in the digital age.[17]

By then, our advocacy efforts on human rights and the Internet in the Universal Periodic Review process were bearing fruit. From small beginnings in 2011, the HRC now had significant evidence of Internet-related human rights violations affecting a wide range of rights: freedom of expression and opinion, privacy, freedom of association, freedom from violence, the right to education and participation in public life, and protection of human rights defenders, particularly those working on media, gender and sexuality.[18]

Pillay's subsequent in-depth investigation of the right to privacy in the digital age was groundbreaking.[19] Governments were obliged to respond to her questions, placing them under pressure to justify their actions according to international human rights standards. Civil society groups knew that these standards had not kept pace with the emerging human rights issues as governments rapidly developed new communications surveillance capabilities, the ability to combine and organise information gained from different surveillance techniques, or the increased sensitivity of information available for governments to access. In 2012, for example, the Electronic Frontier Foundation worked with over 100 legal, human rights and technical experts to develop a specific set of 13 principles articulating how international human rights law applied to the use of technologies for state surveillance.[20]

Digital Age?', 20.09.2013 <https://newsarchive.ohchr.org/EN/NewsEvents/Pages/DisplayNews.aspx?NewsID=13758&LangID=E> accessed 13.07.2020.

16 United Nations General Assembly, 'The Right to Privacy in the Digital Age', GA Res. 68/167, UN GAOR, 3rd Comm., 68th sess., 70th plen. mtg., Agenda Item 69(b), A/RES/68/167, 21.01.2014, adopted 18.12.2013.

17 United Nations Human Rights Council 'Panel on the Right to Privacy in the Digital Age', decision 25/117, A/HRC/DEC27/117, paras. 1–3.

18 By 2014, civil society groups from Association for Progressive Communications networks had filed reports detailing Internet-related human rights issues in 16 countries from all global regions (APC Annual Report 2015), <https://www.apc.org/en/ar2015> accessed 06.03.2021.

19 N. PILLAY, The Right to Privacy in the Digital Age: Report of the Office of the High Commissioner for Human Rights, United Nations, Geneva 2014, A/HRC/27/37.

20 K. RODRIGUEZ, 'Internet Surveillance and Free Speech: The United Nations Makes the Connection', Electronic Frontier Foundation, 04.06.2013 <https://www.eff.org/deeplinks/2013/06/internet-and-surveillance-UN-makes-the-connection> accessed 08.07.2020.

These principles were a good example of how earlier communication rights advocacy strategies were helpful for the progress of Internet-related rights in the international human rights system. On the specific issue of surveillance, the 13 principles provided detailed guidance on the lawfulness of state action, namely that it must be necessary to achieve a lawful purpose, narrowly targeted, and proportionate to its purpose, in line with international human rights standards and norms. By mid-2013, the draft principles were well advanced and, when the revelations broke, these were quickly released more widely.[21] Hundreds of prominent organisations and academics signed on to endorse them, and the principles were used in litigation, legislation, and administrative and advocacy campaigns.[22]

Pillay was able to draw on this, and other work, in her investigation, and was clear and unequivocal in her conclusions.[23] Applying a simple human rights analysis, the report found that all the elements of a human rights violation were present: an interference with specific human rights, clear harms from the interference, and available remedies. Citing the European Court of Human Rights decisions that surveillance of communications technologies violated the right to privacy, Pillay concluded that any capture of communications data was a potential interference with privacy, whether or not the data is later used:[24]

> Even the mere possibility of communications information being captured creates an interference with privacy,[25] with a potential chilling effect on rights, including those to free expression and association. The very existence of a mass surveillance programme thus creates an interference with privacy. The onus would be on the State to demonstrate that such interference is neither arbitrary nor unlawful.

This was a significant victory in the struggle for recognition of the Internet as a place for human rights.[26] In another major step forward

---

21 Electronic Frontier Foundation, 'Necessary and Proportionate: International Principles on the Application of Human Rights to Communications Surveillance', July 2013 version. A full list of signatories is available at <https://necessaryandproportionate.org/sign> accessed 09.07.2020.

22 Electronic Frontier Foundation, '13 Principles: A Legal Toolkit for Global Surveillance Reform' <https://www.eff.org/issues/surveillance-human-rights> accessed 09.07.2020.

23 The full list of submissions is available at <https://www.ohchr.org/EN/Issues/DigitalAge/Pages/ReportDigitalAge.aspx> accessed 09.07.2020.

24 N. PILLAY, above n. 19, para. 20.

25 See *Weber and Saravia v. Germany*, Case No. 54934/00, para. 78; *Malone v United Kingdom*, [1984] ECHR 10, para. 64.

26 See also, e.g. D. JOYCE, 'Privacy in the Digital Era: Human Rights Online?' (2015) 16(1) *Melbourne Journal of International Law*, 270, 282–86.

for the Internet community, the report also concluded that effectively addressing the challenges of the right to privacy in the context of modern technologies would require the adoption of a process of multi-stakeholder engagement.[27] Following the release of the report, and in yet another groundbreaking move, the HRC agreed to create a new human rights mandate: a Special Rapporteur on the Right to Privacy.[28] The first such Special Rapporteur, Professor Joe Cannataci, of Malta, was appointed in July 2015.[29]

4. THE INTERNET GOVERNANCE RESPONSE

The technical and Internet governance communities were watching these developments closely. Appalled by the extent of the vast programme of surveillance, and private sector compliance with orders of secret courts, many were also deeply concerned about the calls to control the Internet. In the complex, interactive Internet governance ecosystem, no stakeholder had any plans to give up their role in making the Internet work: on the contrary, most wanted to ensure, more than ever, that governments alone could never take control of the Internet.

But there were numerous loud demands that 'something be done', from both within and outside the Internet community, and many were feeling the pressure. Governments, especially in Brazil and Germany, but also in many developing countries, were fed up with the geopolitics between other countries, and there were real risks that governments would move to break up the Internet by creating their own national networks, or attempting to take over the organisations in the technical community that made the Internet work. Discussion about the evolution of Internet governance had been under way for years: in particular, to move ICANN away from its place in the US government and onto a truly international footing. Such discussions had never really gained traction, much to the frustration of many in the technical community and elsewhere. The International Telecommunication Union's proposal for a new role for governments, made at the World Telecommunication/ICT Policy Forum in May 2013, was gaining traction, and there was a very real possibility that the idea of

---

27 Above n. 18, para. 49.

28 United Nations Human Rights Council, 'The Right to Privacy in the Digital Age', 01.04.2015, A/HRC/RES/28/16.

29 See <https://www.ohchr.org/EN/Issues/Privacy/SR/Pages/SRPrivacyIndex.aspx> accessed 09.07.2020.

a multi-stakeholder Internet governance community would be sidelined completely.[30]

Tensions were, therefore, running high at the eighth IGF in Bali, soon after the revelations broke. Shortly before the IGF, the main organisations involved in Internet infrastructure broke their silence and issued a statement in response to the revelations about NSA surveillance. The Internet Engineering Task Force, the Internet Architecture Board, the Internet Society, ICANN, the five regional Internet registries, and the World Wide Web Consortium issued the Montevideo Statement in which they:[31]

- expressed strong concern over the recent revelations of pervasive surveillance which had undermined trust and confidence in the Internet, and reinforced the importance of a single global Internet, warning against Internet fragmentation at national level;
- identified the need to reinvigorate Internet governance towards evolution of global coordination among stakeholders;
- called for acceleration of the globalisation of ICANN and Internet Assigned Numbers Authority (IANA) functions, towards an environment where all stakeholders participated on an equal footing; and
- called for transition from Internet Protocol version 4 to version 6 (IPv4 to IPv6) to facilitate a more secure Internet for users.

Coming from such esteemed organisations, the call to accelerate globalisation of ICANN's functions was dramatic and controversial. In doing so, one commentator said, the core Internet institutions had 'turned their back on the US government', with the result that 'the future evolution of Internet name and number governance, at the very least, is no longer up to them'.[32] Fadi Chehadé, chief executive of ICANN, went further, creating a new group named 1net, and boldly travelling to Brazil to seek an audience with President Dilma Rousseff. Rumour had it that

[30] Internet Governance Forum, '8th Meeting of the Internet Governance Forum: Chair's Summary', Bali, Indonesia, 22–25.10.2013, pp. 2–5 <https://www.intgovforum.org/multilingual/content/igf-2013> accessed 06.03.2021.

[31] ICANN, 'The Montevideo Statement' 07.10.2013 <https://www.icann.org/news/announcement-2013-10-07-en> accessed 15.07.2020.

[32] M. MUELLER, 'The Core Internet Institutions Abandon the US Government', Internet Governance Project, Georgia Tech School of Public Policy, 11.10.2013 <https://www.internetgovernance.org/2013/10/11/the-core-internet-institutions-abandon-the-us-government/> accessed 15.07.2020.

the President kept him waiting for some time, but their eventual meeting resulted in agreement for a new global multi-stakeholder meeting, NETmundial, to take place in Brazil in early 2014.[33] The meeting would consider two issues: Internet governance principles and a road map for future evolution of 'the Internet governance ecosystem'.[34]

On the opening day of NETmundial, the president signed into law the Marco de Civil da Internet, the Brazilian code of Internet rights, previously heralded as the global standard in cooperative multi-stakeholder national Internet regulation.[35] NETmundial produced a set of principles, a significant aspect of which was acceptance by all stakeholders (including the private sector) of the HRC resolution that the same 'rights that are protected offline must be protected online in accordance with international legal obligations'.[36] This included the Covenant on Civil and Political Rights (ICCPR), the Covenant on Economic, Cultural and Social Rights (CESCR), and the Convention on the Rights of Persons with Disabilities (CRPD).

The NETmundial agreement was met with cautious optimism, but subsequent attempts to create a new joint initiative with permanent seats for founders in Brazil and in ICANN (and to be hosted by the World Economic Forum) failed.[37] The initiative eventually ground to a halt, in part because of concerns that it would supplant the IGF and other existing multi-stakeholder initiatives. But, in a significant sign that the worlds of the Internet and human rights were converging, the UN General Assembly cited the NETmundial meeting in its resolution calling on the HRC to consider establishing a Special Rapporteur on the Right to Privacy.[38] There could be no mistake: the international human rights system and the Internet were now clearly and inextricably linked.

---

33 'NETmundial (the Global Multi-Stakeholder Meeting on Global Internet Governance)', 24.04.2014 <https://icannwiki.org/NETmundial> accessed 13.07.2020.

34 ibid., p. 2.

35 See the discussion of this in Chapter 4, section 2.1.2 and in Chapter 5, section 4.

36 NETmundial 'NETmundial Multistakholder Statement' para. 2 <https://netmundial.br/netmundial-multistakeholder-statement/> accessed 06.03.2021.

37 J. POHLE, 'Multistakeholderism Unmasked: How the NetMundial Initiative Shifts Battlegrounds in internet governance', *Global Policy*, 05.01.2015 <https://www.globalpolicyjournal.com/blog/05/01/2015/multistakeholderism-unmasked-how-netmundial-initiative-shifts-battlegrounds> accessed 13.07.2020.

38 United Nations General Assembly Resolution on the Right to Privacy in the Digital Age, A/RES/69/166, 14.12.2014, p. 2 and para. 6, p. 4. See also <https://news.un.org/en/story/2013/12/458232-general-assembly-backs-right-privacy-digital-age> accessed 14.12.2020.

Evidence of the influence of human rights on the technical operation of the Internet also emerged elsewhere. Led by the efforts of Niels ten Oever from Article 19, Joana Varon from Coding Rights, and Corinne Cath from the Oxford Internet Institute, the Internet Engineering Task Force (IETF) established a new Human Rights Protocol Considerations Research Group.[39] The Group was chartered to:

> research whether standards and protocols can enable, strengthen or threaten human rights, as defined in the Universal Declaration of Human Rights (UDHR) and the International Covenant on Civil and Political Rights (ICCPR), specifically, but not limited to the right to freedom of expression and the right to freedom of assembly. The research group takes as its starting point the problem statement that human-rights-enabling characteristics of the Internet might be degraded if they are not properly defined, described and sufficiently taken into account in protocol development. Not protecting these characteristics could result in (partial) loss of functionality and connectivity.

The IETF issued new guidance on privacy,[40] as well as Internet blocking and filtering.[41] Their memo RFC 7745, for example, set out detailed descriptions of filtering practices (from firewalls to deep packet inspection and domain name seizures), and the purposes, both lawful and unlawful, and relative effectiveness of each method.

In the process of transitioning to a new international footing, away from US government oversight, ICANN introduced a new human rights by-law to its articles of incorporation.[42] While doubts remain about the extent of ICANN's commitment to implementing this, the reality was that ICANN was now talking about international human rights.[43] This new

---

39 For a brief summary, see A. DORIA, 'Exploring the Impact of Internet Protocols and Architecture on Human Rights', Association for Progressive Communications, 26.03.2019 <https://www.apc.org/en/news/exploring-impact-internet-protocols-and-architectures-human-rights> accessed 23.07.2020.

40 Internet Engineering Task Force, 'RFC 6973: Privacy Considerations for Internet Protocols', July 2013, available at <https://tools.ietf.org/html/rfc6973#page-5> accessed 15.02.2020.

41 Internet Architecture Board, 'RFC 7745: Technical Considerations for Internet Service Blocking and Filtering', March 2016 <https://www.rfc-editor.org/info/rfc7754> accessed 15.07.2020.

42 Bylaws for Internet Corporation for Assigned Names and Numbers, Article 1.2.(b) (viii), as amended 01.10.2016, available at <https://www.icann.org/resources/pages/governance/bylawsen> accessed 15.07.2020.

43 M. ZALNIERIUTE, 'Human Rights Rhetoric in Global Internet Governance: New ICANN Bylaw on Human Rights', [2020] *University of New South Wales Law Research Series*, 6.

by-law, and surrounding work, were thanks in large part to ICANN's Non-Commercial Users Constituency, which championed the initiative, and whose members included human rights defenders with strong links to international human rights organisations.[44] By 2020, ICANN was even readying itself to strengthen privacy protections in order to comply with the EU's General Data Protection Regulation (GDPR).[45]

5. THE EMERGENCE OF HUMAN RIGHTS IN THE DIGITAL AGE

Tensions between the openness and freedom of the Internet were not new, having permeated the creation and evolution of the Internet, and its various uses by human rights defenders and Internet activists. Revelations of global mass surveillance, along with carefully laid groundwork to develop the right to privacy in the digital age, led to fundamental change. The politics that had infused active resistance to the incorporation of human rights principles into the coordination of Internet infrastructure, in organisations such as ICANN, shifted. The UN HRC was now actively engaged with human rights and the Internet, but the discourse in this area was moving away from Internet rights to a new discourse about human rights in the digital age. In this discourse, the application of human rights to a variety of technologies was developing in relation to the use of mobile phones, laptops, desktop personal computers, and the recently developed tablets. While each of these technologies relied on Internet connectivity to one degree or another, the concept of 'Internet rights' seemed an inadequate way to describe the full array of technology-related human rights issues and the language was changing. Navi Pillay, for instance, referred to 'human rights in the digital age' and 'the right to privacy in the digital age', rather than to 'Internet rights'. This emphasised the new way of thinking about the Internet and human rights and the new context in which human rights standards must be respected and protected.

However, the concept of a 'digital age' was bemusing to those familiar with Internet-related technologies because the term had little

---

44 For examples of work by members of the Non-Commercial Users Constituency, see 'Human Rights and Social Responsibility' <https://www.ncuc.org/cause/human-rights/> accessed 15.07.2020.

45 This work includes development of the Registration Data Access Protocol (RDAP), which is expected to replace the WHOIS protocol: see <https://www.icann.org/resources/pages/rdap-faqs-2018-08-31-en> accessed 14.12.2020.

relevance to how the Internet worked. Did 'digital' refer to satellite-based communications? If so, this could be misleading, since it would capture other forms of satellite communication, such as radio and television, that were fundamentally different from the Internet, and already regulated. Or was 'digital' a reference to cellular technologies and, if so, how did this relate to cable-based Internet connectivity? Did the term refer to technologies that collect and transmit data through a binary system of 1s and 0s? Did it mean all of these things and more, such as Wi-Fi-enabled devices? Ultimately, the term was used without prescriptive definition.[46] Perhaps the term was simply a useful rhetorical flourish, suitably evocative – for those unfamiliar with the Internet – of the new context in which human rights issues were arising.

The debate about the right to privacy in the digital age led to new developments elsewhere in the international human rights system. Inspired by Pillay's leadership, and the success of working with one Special Rapporteur, activists began working with others, leading to surges in the number of reports to the HRC about Internet-related interferences, and the number of HRC resolutions.[47] For example, the HRC resolution on human rights and the Internet encouraged 'special procedures to take these issues into account within their existing mandates, as applicable',[48] and many did so.[49]

The Connect Your Rights campaign was still going, focussing on the newly created mandates on the right to privacy and freedom of association, as well as the regional human rights mechanisms, notably in the Inter-American and African regions. New capacity-building initiatives developed, such as the first African Internet governance school, in

---

46 N. PILLAY, above n. 19, p. 3, paras. 1–4.

47 There were eight UN resolutions relating to human rights and the Internet by early 2014: A/HRC/RES/20/8 (The Promotion, Protection and Enjoyment of Human Rights on the Internet); A/RES/68/167 (The Right to Privacy in the Digital Age); A/RES/68/198 (Information and Communications Technologies for Development); A/HRC/RES/21/12 (Safety of Journalists); A/HRC/RES/21/16 (The Rights to Freedom of Peaceful Assembly and of Association); A/HRC/RES/2C3/2 (The Role of Freedom of Opinion and Expression in Women's Empowerment); A/HRC/RES/24/5 (The Rights to Freedom of Peaceful Assembly and of Association); and A/RES/68/243 (Developments in the Field of Information and Telecommunications in the Context of International Security).

48 UNHRC, 'The Promotion, Protection and Enjoyment of Human Rights on the Internet' A/HRC/RES/20/8, 14.07.2014, para. 8.

49 For example, the Special Rapporteurs on Violence against Women, on Protection of Cultural Heritage, and on Freedom of Peaceful Assembly and Association.

Durban, South Africa, which was still going in 2020.[50] The effects of these developments in the international human rights system were eventually seen in some national courts as well. For example, despite the surprising lack of scholarship on Internet shutdowns,[51] the High Court of Islamabad ruled that mobile cellular shutdowns affecting the Internet in Pakistan were unconstitutional.[52]

Finally, as human rights organisations gained deeper understanding of the Internet as a space for human rights, discussion about human rights online, rather than Internet rights, emerged. In this context, proposed new rights also emerged. On the question of a right to encryption, for example, Gus Hosein, executive director of Privacy International, observed that those governments complaining about 'going dark' were doing so despite the fact that they were living, in their own words, in the 'golden age of surveillance'.[53] Now, it could be argued that the right for human rights defenders to use encryption was essential to uphold the rule of law: after all, if governments and the private sector were not going to abide by the rule of law, what incentive was there for civil society and other actors to do so? More importantly, how else were they to defend themselves?

A fundamental transformation of the right to privacy and the concept of human rights in the digital age had taken place with surprising results: human rights defenders were defending the Internet, and the technical community had become human rights defenders.

---

50 African School on Internet Governance <https://afrisig.org/> accessed 15.07.2020.

51 For an excellent study of Internet shutdowns, see B. WAGNER, 'Understanding Internet Shutdowns: A Case Study from Pakistan' *International Journal of Communication*, 12 (2018) 3917.

52 *C M Pak Limited v The PTA and others*, High Court of Islamabad, FAO 42-2016, Hon. Minallah J.

53 G. HOSEIN, 'Introduction' in *Global Information Society Watch 2014: Communications Surveillance in the Digital Age*, Association for Progressive Communications and Hivos, 2014, pp. 9–10 <https://www.giswatch.org/2014-communications-surveillance-digital-age> accessed 05.03.2021.

CHAPTER 7

HUMAN RIGHTS AND THE INTERNET IN A TIME OF COVID-19

1. INTRODUCTION

Contact tracing. QR codes. Bluetooth digital proximity tracing. Fast-forward five years, and our global lexicon is changing as the novel Coronavirus (Covid-19), becomes a pandemic spreading rapidly across the world. Humanity is scrambling to cope, and if there was ever a time for the combined efforts of the technology and human rights communities, it is now. Applying the same human rights offline and online sounds simple: doing so, as outlined in previous chapters, can be messy, complicated, intense, confusing and even fractious. Yet, as the pandemic spreads, something incredible is happening, something that would never have seemed possible back in 2010: human rights online and offline are a critical part of responding to a global health crisis. This chapter explores some of the tensions that emerged – between human rights and technology design, between conflicting rights to privacy and health, and between regulatory responses – and how human rights, science and technical communities responded to those tensions in rights-affirming ways.

2. COVID-19

According to the World Health Organization (WHO), coronaviruses are a large family of viruses that can cause illness in animals or humans. In humans, several of these coronaviruses cause respiratory infections, ranging from the common cold to more severe diseases such as Middle East respiratory syndrome (MERS) and severe acute respiratory syndrome (SARS).[1] In December 2019, a new coronavirus caused a new type of coronavirus disease: Covid-19.

We may never know exactly how the outbreak began, but this much appears agreed on by reputable medical and scientific organisations. In late 2019, news of an undiagnosed illness began emerging from Wuhan, China. On 31 December 2019, Chinese national authorities informed the WHO China Country Office of cases of pneumonia with an unknown cause. The clinical signs were 'mainly fever, with a few patients having difficulty in breathing and chest radiographs showing invasive lesions of both lungs'.[2] By 3 January 2020, there were 44 reported cases, 11 of whom were severely ill, while 33 were in a stable condition. The Wuhan Municipal Health Commission initiated a public health response, carrying out a range of measures, including active case finding, tracing close contacts of patients, and environmental hygiene investigations.[3] On 30 January, when there were fewer than 100 cases in China and no reported deaths, the Director-General of the WHO, Dr Tedros Adhanom Ghebreyesus, declared a public health emergency of international concern. During February, four countries emerged as having high case numbers and associated illness and deaths: China, Iran, Italy and Spain. Less than six weeks later, on 11 March, Dr Ghebreyesus took the historic step of announcing a global pandemic: cases outside China had grown thirteen-fold, and there were reports of more than 118,000 cases in 114 countries, thousands in hospital, and 4,291 deaths.[4]

In New Zealand, we were following developments closely. Despite being an island nation with a population of 5 million, at the southern edge of the Pacific Ocean, it was clear that transmission was only a matter of time. The first case was reported on 28 February: a person in their 60s who had recently returned from Iran.[5] All borders and entry points were closed

---

1 World Health Organization, 'What is a Coronavirus?: Q&A on Coronaviruses – Covid19' (2019) <https://www.who.int/emergencies/diseases/novel-coronavirus-2019/question-and-answers-hub/q-a-detail/q-a-coronaviruses> accessed 17.08.2020.

2 World Health Organization, 'Pneumonia of Unknown Cause – China', Disease Outbreak News, 05.01.2020 <https://www.who.int/csr/don/05-january-2020-pneumonia-of-unkown-cause-china/en/> accessed 18.08.2020.

3 ibid.

4 World Health Organization, 'WHO Director-General's Opening Remarks at the Media Briefing on COVID-19, March 2020', 11.03.2020 <https://www.who.int/dg/speeches/detail/who-director-general-s-opening-remarks-at-the-media-briefing-on-covid-19---11-march-2020> accessed 17.08.2020.

5 Ministry of Health, New Zealand, 'Single Case of Covid-19 Confirmed in New Zealand', 28.02.2020 <https://www.health.govt.nz/news-media/media-releases/single-case-covid-19-confirmed-new-zealand> accessed 18.08.2020.

to non-New Zealand residents or citizens on 19 March, and all returnees were required to spend two weeks in managed isolation.

Just as other countries began national lockdowns, so too in New Zealand the decision was made to close down public places and ask people to stay at home. On 21 March, the prime minister, Jacinda Ardern, announced a nationwide four-level alert system.[6] On 23 March, there were 36 new cases, bringing the total number to 102,[7] and the country was placed on Alert Level 3 ('there is a high risk that the disease is not contained and community transmission might be happening').[8] At midnight on 25 March, New Zealand entered Level 4 ('it is likely that the disease is not contained, community transmission is occurring and there are widespread outbreaks and clusters'). New Zealanders were asked to stay at home and maintain contact only with people in their family or household 'bubble'.[9] All public gatherings (including funerals) were cancelled, all schools and businesses closed, except for those deemed essential, and all but essential travel was restricted.

Jacinda Ardern urged the nation's 'team' of 5 million to 'be strong, be kind'.[10] Streets emptied, businesses closed, hospital staff and healthcare workers readied themselves, supermarket workers stocked shelves, and public health experts encouraged us that collective action really could save lives. Our 'team' of five million stayed at home; together with the rest of the world, we waited.

3. THE IMPORTANCE OF THE INTERNET

Debate about the right to privacy in the digital age, as we saw in Chapter 6, was characterised by shocking media revelations, public dismay, human rights advocacy, and governmental geopolitics about control of the Internet. Then, it was as if a slumbering global public, suddenly awakened to the implications of their online lives, had been shocked by what they saw: the evil potential of the Internet suddenly revealed, the science fiction panopticon made real.

6 See <https://covid19.govt.nz/alert-system/alert-system-overview/> accessed 06.03.2021.

7 Ministry of Health, New Zealand, '36 New Cases of Covid-19 in New Zealand' 23.03.2020 <https://www.health.govt.nz/news-media/media-releases/36-new-cases-covid-19-new-zealand> accessed 18.08.2020.

8 Office of the Prime Minister, New Zealand, 'New Zealand Moves to Alert Level 3, then Level 4 in 48 Hours', 23.03.2020 <https://www.beehive.govt.nz/release/new-zealand-moves-covid-19-alert-level-3-then-level-4-48-hours> accessed 18.08.2020.

9 The legality of these instructions was the subject of litigation in *Borrowdale v Director-General of Health* [2020] NZHC 2090, Thomas, Venning and Ellis JJ.

10 ibid.

Debate about the Internet in the time of the global Covid-19 pandemic could hardly be more different. As governments began issuing public health directives to stay at home, Internet access became critical for millions of people, and a vital public health defence line for governments. Internet related public health needs included: finding and sharing the latest pandemic news, broadcasting national updates and travel alerts, and advising the public on new business rules and which services were open or closed. For the public, Internet access was critical, not only for receiving information, but also for fulfilling simple human needs to communicate with family and friends; to live, love, explore and play in a new communal *online* way. During the pandemic, the Internet finally emerged as a space in its own right: a place where we truly live.

This was apparent in the incredible outpourings of solidarity with 'front line' health workers – nurses, doctors and other medical professionals, and with cleaners, supermarket workers, rubbish collectors, residential care workers and police. Who can forget the moving sight of people gathering in their doorways or front yards to applaud, light a candle, sing, or simply stand in silence for a few moments to honour those workers, and those dead or dying? Or the uplifting images from Italy of a gym instructor giving rooftop fitness classes to residents of apartment blocks; of Spanish musicians playing to elderly rest home residents gathered cautiously on their balconies; of neighbours singing to each other across streets and buildings, just to keep their spirits up. These, and thousands of other acts of solidarity and courage, travelled around the world within minutes. The power of the Internet was palpable, and people were harnessing it in new and incredible ways for the collective good.

In New Zealand, as in many other countries, the Internet was at the centre of both government pandemic responses and the daily coping strategies of individuals and groups. For children and young people, the Internet was critical for accessing education and keeping in contact with teachers and school communities. For people working from home, Internet access enabled remote working. For employers and business owners, especially those who had previously been reluctant to enable remote working, the Internet was essential to keep their businesses going. Demand for online videoconferencing tools skyrocketed, and some, such as Zoom, struggled to cope with the surge in demand.[11] New language

[11] J. WAKEFIELD, 'Zoom Boss Apologises for Security Issues and Promises Fixes', 02.04.2020 <https://www.bbc.com/news/technology-52133349> accessed 18.08.2020.

emerged, as people used the Internet and other technologies to 'pivot' into new ways of working.

The pandemic was also highlighting entrenched social, cultural, economic and digital divides, the vulnerability of women to domestic violence, and the plight of those without housing. Globally, new human rights issues emerged for the vulnerable and marginalised, and those living in refugee camps or experiencing the effects of a rise in xenophobia and discrimination. Human rights groups called on governments to release political prisoners or provide them with proper aid, to prevent outbreaks of Covid-19 in jails. In Egypt, for example, our brother Alaa Abd El-Fattah went on hunger strike to protest against restrictions on family visits to prisoners which prevented his mother from providing him with medical supplies.[12] We could support all of these causes in solidarity because of Internet access.

As the situation rapidly evolved, there were calls for technology-related solutions; symptom-tracking apps, digital contact tracing apps and immunity passports apps came under particular consideration. I followed the issue of digital proximity contact tracing closely, and was surprised by the maturity, sophistication and speed of the human rights analyses, something that I would have thought improbable even a few years before.

4. DIGITAL PROXIMITY CONTACT TRACING

'Contact tracing' refers to the practice of identifying and isolating people exposed to an infectious disease. The purpose of contact tracing is to prevent the ongoing transmission of a disease by identifying and isolating people who test positive for the disease as part of an overall response to trace, test and quarantine or voluntarily self-isolate all people who have been in close contact with them. Most public health contact tracing is manual: people interviewing people who test positive to find out where they have been and identify all of their possible close contacts. While this is effective, the fallibility of human memory and the labour-intensive nature of manual contact tracing hamper its speed. It may be difficult for a person to accurately recall all the places they have been, and all others they have had contact with, especially if they are unwell and stressed.

---

12 Middle East Eye, 'Jailed Egyptian Activist Alaa Abdel Fattah Ends Hunger Strike', 19.05.2020 <https://www.middleeasteye.net/news/jailed-egyptian-activist-alaa-abdel-fattah-ends-hunger-strike> accessed 18.08.2020.

With the advent of new technologies, digital contact tracing options have developed, some of which are already in use, or have been trialled in the last ten years, including in Ebola, MERS and SARS outbreaks.[13] As the Covid-19 pandemic grew, so too did concern that manual contact tracing might be too slow to reach people before they were aware they were transmitting the disease. Modelling exercises carried out by researchers concluded that the speed and scalability of digital options using proximity sensors in smartphones was, theoretically, fast enough to stop spread of the disease if used by enough people, and in combination with other measures such as physical distancing.[14] In April 2020, a team at the University of Oxford used epidemiological modelling to help configure a contact tracing app for the virus, and openly shared the results. The team noted that 'development of an app needs a technological component and an epidemiological component', because a technological solution 'is necessary but not sufficient to secure its success'.[15] Using a set of assumptions (including a user's self-diagnosis), the team concluded that the epidemic could be suppressed if 80 per cent of the UK's smartphone users used the app, or 56 per cent of the overall population.[16]

As calls to use digital technologies grew louder, three main options emerged, each with its own risks and challenges: geolocation, Bluetooth and QR Codes.

4.1. GEOLOCATION

Geolocation uses software that usually runs in the background of smartphones to support services such as Google Maps. Typically,

---

13 A. ANGLEMYER et al, 'Digital Contact Tracing in Epidemics: A Rapid Review' (2020) *Cochrane Database of Systemic Reviews*, Issue 8, Art. No: CD013699 <https://www.cochranelibrary.com/cdsr/doi/10.1002/14651858.CD013699/epdf/full> accessed 24.08.2020.

14 L. FERETTI et al, 'Quantifying SARS-CoV-2 Transmission Suggests Epidemic Control with Digital Contact Tracing – Research Article Summary' (2020) *Science*, Vol. 368, 619.

15 R. HINCH et al, 'Effective Configurations of a Digital Contact Tracing App: A report to NHSX', University of Oxford, 16.04.2020, p. 1 <https://045.medsci.ox.ac.uk/files/files/report-effective-app-configurations.pdf> accessed 06.03.2021 and see also this summary of the research University of Oxford, 'Digital Contact Tracing can Slow or even Stop Coronavirus Transmission and Ease Us out of Lockdown' 16.04.2020, <https://www.research.ox.ac.uk/Article/2020-04-16-digital-contact-tracing-can-slow-or-even-stop-coronavirus-transmission-and-ease-us-out-of-lockdown> accessed 24.08.2020.

16 R. HINCH et al, above n. 15, p. 3.

geolocation uses mobile phone network data, Global Positioning System (GPS) data and Wi-Fi signals to track people to within about ten metres of their location.

Taiwanese authorities used geolocation data analysis to support rapid contact tracing to identify people who had been in contact with over 3,000 people who had disembarked the Diamond Princess cruise ship in Keelong Harbour on 31 January 2020, five days before the index case on the ship was identified. Using big data analytics, combined with CCTV footage, credit card usage data and public transport information, authorities were able to identify 627,386 possible contacts, even though the ship had been in harbour for only one day. Authorities sent SMS messages to all of those identified, providing public health information on how to mitigate spread of the disease, and offering testing to anyone who had symptoms. Of the 67 people tested, all were negative.[17] Researchers concluded that big data analytics, when combined with smart contact tracing, automated text alerts, self-quarantine, and follow-up using national health insurance information, could enable 'successful prevention of community spread of COVID-19'.[18]

4.2. BLUETOOTH

Bluetooth is the technology that enables devices to connect with each other via a 'digital handshake'. Bluetooth can work on devices up to a metre apart, and is much more accurate than geolocation because it works by measuring signal strength between two devices, such as a computer and keyboard. As the pandemic spread, researchers began discussing the possibilities of digital contact tracing using Bluetooth-enabled devices, such as smartphones, to assess whether their users had been in close enough proximity to spread the virus.

Singapore was the first country to develop a digital proximity contact tracing app using Bluetooth: TraceTogether.[19] Other countries quickly followed such as Malaysia's MyTrace, and Vietnam's Bluezone. In Australia,

---

17 C-M. CHEN et al, 'Containing COVID-19 Among 627,386 Persons in Contact With the Diamond Princess Cruise Ship Passengers Who Disembarked in Taiwan: Big Data Analytics', *Journal of Medical Internet Research* (2020); 22(5):e19540 <https://www.jmir.org/2020/5/e19540> accessed 26.08.2020.

18 ibid., 8.

19 The Singaporean app is available at <https://www.tracetogether.gov.sg/> accessed 20.08.2020.

the COVIDSafe app uses Bluetooth to record an encrypted handshake between phones that are within the virus's transmission range of one another. Once the app is installed and operational, users simply need to carry their phones when travelling outside of their homes.[20]

4.3. QR CODES

A QR (quick response) code is a machine-readable label that contains information about an item, such as an address (online or physical), text (such as contact details), or product or content information. First developed in the mid-1990s in the Japanese car industry, today QR codes can be easily scanned using mobile phones, and are used for a wide variety of purposes, including ticketing for entertainment or transport, making payments, and logging into websites. QR codes can be used, on almost any object or building, to transmit (via Wi-Fi networks) geolocation information, and any other information they might contain.

QR Codes have been applied in a wide variety of ways to assist Covid-19 contact tracing. In New Zealand, for example, all businesses and public premises are required to register and display unique QR codes, which visitors scan upon entry, creating a digital diary to assist with manual contact tracing. In China, QR codes displayed in public places, such as bus and train stations, have been integrated with smartphone apps. Once users can self-assess their risk of Covid-19, the app generates a colour-coded health status (green, orange or red) that determines the passenger's status to travel.[21]

4.4. DISCUSSION

The rise in digital proximity contact tracing generated an 'apps race' – the first 'appification' of a pandemic crisis response. By early July 2020, Covid-19 Digital Rights Tracker reported 80 apps in 50 countries, 35 per cent of which

---

[20] B. HOWELL, 'A Tale of Two Contact Tracing Apps: Lessons from Australia and New Zealand', American Enterprise Institute blog, 22.05.2020 <https://www.aei.org/technology-and-innovation/a-tale-of-two-contact-tracing-apps-lessons-from-australia-and-new-zealand/> accessed 28.08.2020.

[21] S. ANKEL, 'As China Lifts its Coronavirus Lockdowns, Authorities are Using a Colour-coded Health System to Dictate where Citizens can Go. Here's how it Works', Business Insider, 08.04.2020 <https://www.businessinsider.com.au/coronavirus-china-health-software-color-coded-how-it-works-2020-4?r=US&IR=T> accessed 18.09.2020.

were using Bluetooth, 34 per cent GPS, and 24 per cent a combination of both. There were 35 countries using alternative methods.[22]

The development and deployment of these apps has been characterised by vigorous public debate about human rights; a debate supported, in general, by high-quality research about the benefits and significant limitations of digital proximity contact tracing.[23]

The speed of critical human rights analysis seems to be increasing. As quickly as research on epidemiological and technical aspects of digital proximity contact tracing was published, academics from around the globe share research about various human rights implications of proposed technology responses.[24] For example, there are significant interdisciplinary collaborations between academics and activists throughout Europe, Asia, Africa and Latin America.

The time lag between human rights critique and technology development is definitely closing. I could see this in discussion of the two primary deployment options for digital proximity contact tracing apps: centralised versus decentralised. Each option raises different technology and human rights issues, and new collaborations have quickly formed as experts in a wide range of disciplines identify human rights, health, ethical and technical issues.

In a centralised system, the computation of location, proximity to others and risk of infection is done via a back-end server (generally under government control), with each phone sending temporary unique identifiers, and storing those received from nearby phones. Data may be gathered and stored locally on users' phones, then processed by a centrally-located, government-controlled server once a diagnosis confirms

---

22 S. WOODHAMS, 'COVID-19 Digital Rights Tracker', Top10VPN.com <https://www.top10vpn.com>. See also J. LI and X. GUO, 'COVID-19 Contact-tracing Apps: A Survey on the Global Deployment and Challenges', arXiv.org, arXiv:2005.03599, 13.05.2020, p. 4 <https://arxiv.org/abs/2005.03599>, which estimated that Bluetooth accounted for 57% of tracking technologies and GPS 43%.

23 See, e.g. U. GASSER et al, 'Digital Tools against Covid-19: Taxonomy, Ethical Challenges, and Navigation Aid', (2020) *The Lancet Digital Health*, Vol. 2, Issue 8, E425–34 <https://www.thelancet.com/journals/landig/article/PIIS2589-7500(20)30137-0/fulltext> accessed 06.03.2021; R. KLEINMAN and C. MERKEL, 'Digital Contact Tracing for COVID-19' (2020) *Canadian Medical Association Journal* 192(24), E653–56 <https://www.cmaj.ca/content/192/24/E653> accessed 26.08.2020; R. RASKAR et al, 'Apps Gone Rogue: Maintaining Personal Privacy in an Epidemic' arXiv.org <arXiv:2003.08567v1> accessed 26.08.2020.

24 See, e.g. E. M. KUSKONMAZ and E. GUILD, 'Covid-19: A New Struggle over Privacy, Data Protection and Human Rights?', European Law Blog, 04.05.2020 <https://europeanlawblog.eu/2020/05/04/covid-19-a-new-struggle-over-privacy-data-protection-and-human-rights/> accessed 18.08.2020.

infection. For example, the Singapore model estimates the risk of Covid-19 transmission of infection, after an individual diagnosis, by sending the user's locally stored information to a trusted public health authority.[25] Advantages of a centralised system include the ability to link to a person's existing health records, and the low risk of false declarations, since diagnosis is carried out by a health official.

In a decentralised system, information about location, proximity and risk of infection is computed locally on the user's smartphone, with data about specific exposure events, such as a visit or interaction with other people, stored and controlled locally on the user's phone. Decentralised systems put the user in control of when and how they share their information, as well as minimising collection, retention and use of data, and enabling data deletion.

A deep divide soon appeared between technical, private sector, government and human rights experts, over centralised versus decentralised systems. In March 2020, a European collaboration, Pan-European Privacy-Preserving Proximity Tracing, developed software using a centralised back-end system, to support national initiatives.[26] The software was picked up by French, Italian and German governments, and had the support of some national data protection authorities.

However, the Decentralized Privacy-Preserving Proximity Tracing (DP-3T) initiative criticised the Pan-European initiative, releasing an analysis that showed that it had significant privacy and security risks.[27] DP-3T issued its own White Paper on the data needed to support effective digital contact tracing. In this paper, more than 30 experts, including teams of epidemiologists, legal experts, and privacy engineers (people with the skills to enable privacy by design), proposed deployment via decentralised systems as the best way to protect user privacy and support public health responses to the pandemic.[28] The White Paper proposed use of Bluetooth technology on apps to establish proximity to others also using the app, in

25 J. BAY et al, 'BlueTrace: A Privacy-preserving Protocol for Community-driven Contact Tracing across Borders', White Paper, Government Technology Agency, Singapore 2020 <https://bluetrace.io/> accessed 18.09.2020.

26 Pan-European Privacy-Preserving Proximity Tracing (PEPP-PT), 'Data Protection and Security Architecture: Illustrated on the German Implementation' 18.04.2020 <https://github.com/pepp-pt/pepp-pt-documentation/> accessed 18.09.2020.

27 The DP-3T Project, 'Security and Privacy Analysis of the Document 'PEPP-PT: Data Protection and Information Security Architecture' 19.04.2020 <https://github.com/DP-3T/documents/find/master> accessed 18.09.2020.

28 M. SALATHÉ and C. CATTUTO, 'Covid-19 Response: What Data is Necessary for Digital Proximity Tracing?', GitHub, 11.04.2020 <https://github.com/DP-3T/documents/find/master> accessed 18.09.2020.

preference to the use of GPS location information on telecommunication networks, or Bluetooth systems that used centralised back-end systems.

In the private sector, Google and Apple took the unprecedented step of supporting a decentralised privacy-preserving exposure notification system, closely modelled on the DP-3T model, and using Bluetooth in iOS and Android phones. They made this publicly available for developers, including governments, to use.[29] Many welcomed this initiative, although there were concerns about its significant technical limitations. The move was also denounced by some because of the potential reach of US laws that enable US law enforcement agencies to request access to Google and Apple data. This led some governments to reject the initiative. For instance, the French government preferred to assert French data sovereignty by operating StopCovid, its own national centralised system.[30]

As this debate unfolded, so too was there criticism of the technology used to develop and deploy the apps. For example, while proximity tracing is more precise than geolocation, it still has limitations. Bluetooth technology was never designed to track people, and can produce false positive and false negative results when used in this new way.[31] There were concerns about 'function creep', such as the introduction of app use for quarantine control or immunity passports by government authorities, using updates on centralised systems.[32] To avoid this, some countries, such as Switzerland, have pledged to use a decentralised system.[33] The integration of contact-tracing technology into the operating systems of Apple and Android devices also raised due process concerns about how to remove it, the legal grounds for turning the app off, and who can authorise app deletion.

---

29 F. SAINZ, 'Google and Apple Partner on COVID-19 Contact Tracing Technology', Apple Newsroom, 10.04.2020 <https://www.apple.com/newsroom/2020/04/apple-and-google-partner-on-covid-19-contact-tracing-technology/> accessed 06.03.2021.

30 N. MORENO, 'Coronavirus Contact Tracing Apps: Global Privacy Perspective', Lexology, 04.05.2020 <https://www.lexology.com/library/detail.aspx?g=233d958e-c9c9-4044-b61e-b146ff8e291f> accessed 06.03.2021.

31 E. MASSÉ, 'Privacy and Public Health: The Dos and Don'ts for COVID-19 Contact Tracing Apps', Access Now, 04.05.2020 <https://www.accessnow.org/privacy-and-public-health-the-dos-and-donts-for-covid-19-contact-tracing-apps/> accessed 25.08.2020.

32 J. VITAK and M. ZIMMER, 'Using Contextual Integrity to Evaluate the Long-Term Risks from COVID-19 Surveillance Technologies', Social Media and Society, Vol 6, Issue 3, July-September 2020, <ttps://journals.sagepub.com/doi/10.1177/2056305120948250> accessed 06.03.2020.

33 S. IBRAHIM, 'Switzerland issues Covid tracing app for residents' Swiss Info, 25.06.2020 <https://www.swissinfo.ch/eng/business/switzerland-launches-swisscovid-contact-tracing-app-for-residents/45859778> accessed 06.03.2021.

By April 2020, seven out of ten contact-tracing apps were running on centralised systems,[34] but some governments had started to retreat from them. There was evidence of significant limitations with the apps, such as dependencies on high rates of smartphone ownership and app download; a need for continuous, consistent use; and good quality device hardware to enable signal strength (namely, newer model phones). The technologies had weaknesses, such as variations in proximity precision in indoor and outdoor environments, and the limited spatial specificity of barcodes.[35] Many of the apps also had weak privacy protections: of the 80 apps in use, for example, one in five had no privacy policy.[36] By mid-2020, the UK National Health Service's plans to introduce a centralised system based on a trial on the Isle of Wight[37] were shelved following significant criticism.[38] In Singapore, public uptake of the TraceTogether app had reached only 25 per cent, and the country suffered a significant resurgence, leading the government to add a Bluetooth token to the system.[39]

Another feature of the debate about digital proximity tracing apps is the multiple and intersecting human rights identified as being important: the rights to health, privacy, access to and freedom of information, freedom of expression, employment, and economic and social rights. At the intersections of these rights are questions of how to balance them. Is public health more important than the economy? Is the right to privacy more important than the right to health? What are the duties of governments to protect against harm to public health? The questions echo Internet and human rights debates about freedom of expression versus freedom from discrimination, or the right to security versus the right to privacy. In contrast, however, the debate over apps has placed more emphasis on a

---

34 L. CLARKE, 'Seven in Ten Global Covid-19 Contact Tracing Apps Run on a Centralised Model' NS Tech, 22.04.2020 <https://tech.newstatesman.com/security/seven-in-ten-global-covid-19-contact-tracing-apps-run-on-a-centralised-model>.

35 R. KLEINMAN and C. MERKEL, above n. 23.

36 S. WOODHAMS, above n. 22.

37 National Health Service, 'Next Phase of NHS Coronavirus (COVID-19) App Announced', 18.06.2020 <https://www.gov.uk/government/news/next-phase-of-nhs-coronavirus-covid-19-app-announced> accessed 25.08.2020.

38 M. VEALE, 'Analysis of the NHSX Contact Tracing App "Isle of Wight" Data Protection Impact Assessment', LawArXiv, 09.05.2020 <osf.io/preprints/lawarxiv/6fvgh> accessed 25.08.2020.

39 R. NADRAJAN, 'New TraceTogether Token to have no GPS or Internet Connectivity to Track User's Whereabouts: Vivian Balakrishnan', Today Online, 09.06.2020 <https://www.todayonline.com/singapore/tracetogether-token-has-no-gps-or-internet-connectivity-track-users-whereabouts-vivian> accessed 06.03.2021.

holistic approach, weighing all rights and freedoms in the balance, rather than allowing one to trump another.

This holistic, intersectional approach to rights is also evident in discussion about the right to privacy, which has included not only the privacy of infected people, but also of those vulnerable to infection, and even of non-infected people.[40] Broadcasting public health alerts about the locations of outbreaks and probable cases is important to enable testing and isolation. However, such broadcasting also poses risks and challenges for infected people and their families if, for example, their individual homes or apartment blocks are identified, or they have been incorrectly diagnosed. Businesses that have been identified as places where outbreaks have occurred may face ostracism, or be vulnerable to fraud or other exploitation. Providing too much information may also put individuals, workers and communities at risk of discrimination and harassment, both online and offline. While the answers to these issues are not straightforward, this holistic approach to the human rights implications of technology is in contrast to the previous, narrower focus on freedom of expression, freedom of association and privacy.

5. REGULATORY APPROACHES

Digital proximity contact-tracing apps raise profound questions about public trust, legality and functionality: questions in which the Internet is deeply embedded. All apps, for example, rely on Internet access, whether for trialling, downloading, data uploading, data sharing or software updates. This poses challenges for regulatory approaches.

5.1. PUBLIC HEALTH LEGISLATION

Public health legislation in many countries predates the Internet. Even in those countries which do have modern public health law – such as South Korea, which passed the Infectious Disease Prevention Act in 2015 in response to MERS – there is no clear legal authority for widespread surveillance of the non-criminal population for public health purposes.[41]

---

40 R. RASKAR et al, above n. 23.

41 K. S. PARK, Korea University School of Law, 'Statement on Korea', Open Net Korea 2020 <https://opennet.or.kr> accessed 06.03.2021.

Even fewer countries have modern laws governing the use of the Internet and digital technology for such surveillance.

While the UN HRC's response to the right to privacy in the digital age did not anticipate a global pandemic, it helped lay the foundations for today's multi-stakeholder collaborations and initiatives on technology and human rights. Human rights bodies in the UN have reiterated the need for national laws and policies to comply with international human rights standards, even in a public health emergency, and for surveillance technologies to meet the standards of necessity, legitimacy and proportionality.[42]

Human rights standards have also been prominent in the WHO's commentary on contact-tracing apps. For example, the WHO have acknowledged that digital proximity tracing apps have been useful in the pandemic, and in preparing for future responses, but may also threaten fundamental human rights, during and after the pandemic. Since 'surveillance can quickly traverse the blurred line between disease surveillance and population surveillance', the WHO has called for 'laws, policies and oversight' to place 'strict limits on use of proximity tracking technologies and research on data generated by them'.[43] To assist with this, the WHO has developed 17 ethical principles to guide the use of digital proximity tracing. These include minimising data collection to only that which is necessary to achieve a public health objective, restrictions on the use of data, voluntary (rather than compulsory) download and use, privacy-preserving data storage and security, infection reporting and consent protocols, independent oversight, and civil society participation and engagement.

5.2. SPECIFIC DIGITAL CONTACT TRACING LAWS

With public health laws often predating the Internet, the rapidly developing literature and technology on digital contacting tracing apps showed that new laws were needed. Professor Lilian Edwards of Newcastle University's Law School, realising that existing data protection and privacy laws would

---

42 See also the United Nations Human Rights Committee, 'Statement on Derogations from the Covenant in Connection with the COVID-19 Pandemic', 24.04.2020, CCPR/C/128/2.

43 World Health Organization, 'Ethical Considerations to Guide the Use of Digital Proximity Tracking Technologies for COVID-19 contact tracing', Interim Guidance, 28.05.2020, p. 1 <https://www.who.int/publications/i/item/WHO-2019-nCoV-Ethics_Contact_tracing_apps-2020.1> accessed 06.03.2021.

be inadequate, led the development of a model law: 'The Coronavirus (Safeguards) Bill 2020: Proposed protections for digital interventions and in relation to immunity certificates.'[44]

The model law is a remarkable example of the connection between the Internet and human rights. The bill responds, for example, to key human rights concerns for vulnerable and marginalised groups who may not have access to technology, or may be subjected to unfair discrimination or coercion based on the mistaken impression that a contact tracing app would be a suitable proxy for assessing a person's health status. The model law sets out that a person should not be compelled to download the app, to use it in order to access a public place, or to produce it to an employer. Likewise, it provides that a person should not be penalised for not having a mobile phone or, if they do, leaving home without it, or turning off its Bluetooth capability. Other human rights safeguards in the Bill include a requirement to delete data, and a proposed Commissioner to oversee the digital contact tracing system.

In Australia, new and specific digital contact tracing legislation has been introduced,[45] setting out new, technology-specific human rights. It has also introduced a new offence of requiring someone to download the government's Covid-19 app,[46] and offences prohibiting discrimination by employers, or in the provision of goods and services or the imposition of financial conditions, with penalties of up to five years in jail and fines of up to $60,000. The list of permitted health data uses is very narrow, limited to contact tracing, or investigation by police or data commissioners of breaches of the legislation; and statistical use is limited to information on total app registrations only.

While the Australian app collects all contact events (not only those within 1.5 metres for longer than 15 minutes), contact events are only shared with public health contact tracers if the user tests positive for Covid-19. To ensure that this personal information is not shared more widely, and to avoid possible 'scope creep', the Australian law specifically overrides all other powers of law enforcement agencies to demand information. Finally, uploaded logs remain on the system until

---

44 The model law can be found at <https://osf.io/preprints/lawarxiv/yc6xu/> accessed 06.03.2021.

45 Privacy Amendment (Public Health Contact Information) Act 2020 (Australia). For a useful critique, see G. GREENLEAF and K. KEMP, 'Australia's COVIDSafe Experiment, Phase III: Legislation for Trust in Contact Tracing', 15.05.2020, *University of New South Wales Legal Research Series* <https://papers.ssrn.com/sol3/papers.cfm?abstract_id=3601730> accessed 06.03.2021.

46 Amendment (Public Health Contact Information) Act 2020, s. 94(H)(2).

authorities determine that the app is no longer required, or is deemed no longer effective. Thereafter, authorities must delete the app data, remove availability of the app, and tell users to delete it.

It is too soon in the progression of the pandemic to know how well these laws are working in practice, and what other issues may emerge from second, third or rolling, continuous outbreaks. The specific laws needed in any given country may ultimately depend on the degree of public health risk, the overall state of public health, and any culturally specific needs. Regardless of context, all countries are seeking to use similar technologies, and must meet the same human rights standards.

6. IMPLICATIONS

Already, we have gained useful insights that bode well, not only for technological tools for use in combatting the pandemic, but for future Internet and human rights issues. One of these has been the high quality of technology-related human rights analyses, and the speed with which these analyses have been developed and shared. The days of Internet Protocols, the development of new technologies, and human rights standards being far removed from each other seem long ago. The idea that human rights could be technologically neutral, and that standards could apply without specific application to technologies has also moved on: there are new policies and laws that give specific expression to human rights online, and in relation to specific digital technologies.

In addition, in the midst of the pandemic, expertise in human rights online and offline is converging and delivering new and inspiring results. Technical engineers, human rights lawyers, epidemiologists, health practitioners and many other experts are demonstrating that the whole of their collaborations can be greater than the sum of their individual parts, leading to the creation of digital proximity tracing technologies that are human rights-affirming, and which can support public health objectives to slow the Covid-19 pandemic.

At the same time, the pandemic has also revealed the very real limits of technology: there is no 'technological solution' that can replace manual contact tracing.[47] A broader question of effectiveness still hangs over the whole debate: do digital proximity tracing apps really work? The Ada Lovelace Institute, for example, has concluded that there is no clear

[47] World Health Organization, above n. 43.

evidence of digital contact tracing apps actually helping to curb the virus.[48] A literature review published in *The Lancet* went further:[49]

> Of the 4036 studies identified, 110 full-text studies were reviewed and 15 studies were included in the final analysis and quality assessment. No empirical evidence of the effectiveness of automated contact tracing (regarding contacts identified or transmission reduction) was identified .... Large-scale manual contact tracing is therefore still key in most contexts.

The lack of evidence that these apps actually work to prevent transmission is also a sharp reminder that technology is not an end in itself, but needs to work in the service of the public good and have clear public health benefits. One New Zealand expert, for example, recently noted that, when used with other basic public health measures, rapid contact tracing has been shown to have 'over 90% efficacy against Covid-19 disease at the population level, making it as effective as many vaccines'.[50]

While the combination of humans and technology is better than either one alone, many public health systems have struggled to cope with outdated manual contact tracing systems, or with scaling up their manual systems quickly enough (such as by hiring and training new staff). The absence of comprehensive public health infrastructure in the United States, for example, meant that, for one commentator, the race for digital contact tracing was over before it began.[51] And, in what may yet prove to be a haunting irony, the API developed by Apple and Google is not being widely used in the United States.

For now, even a cursory look back at the start of the pandemic shows that the days of wondering what the technical and human rights communities could achieve if they worked together are gone. The 'appification' of the pandemic has revealed tensions: between centralised and decentralised

---

48 Ada Lovelace Institute, 'Rapid Evidence Review: Exit through the App Store?', 20.04.2020 <https://www.adalovelaceinstitute.org/our-work/covid-19/covid-19-exit-through-the-app-store/> accessed 28.08.2020.

49 I. BRAITHWAITE et al, 'Automated and Partly Automated Contact Tracing: A Systematic Review to Inform the Control of COVID-19' (2020) *The Lancet Digital Health*, Vol. 2, Issue 11, E607–21.

50 A. VERRALL, 'Rapid Audit of Contact Tracing for COVID-19 in New Zealand', 10.04.2020, p. 1 <https://www.health.govt.nz/publication/rapid-audit-contact-tracing-covid-19-new-zealand> accessed 28.08.2020.

51 J. ZITTRAIN, 'Is Digital Contact Tracing Over Before It Began?', 16.06.2020 <https://medium.com/berkman-klein-center/is-digital-contact-tracing-over-before-it-began-925c72036ee7> accessed 28.08.2020.

systems (on issues such as which would be best for whom, and why), between privacy and the right to health, and between human rights and technology. These tensions echo themes elsewhere in this book about empowering users at the edges of the Internet, rather than via a single point of control, and the duties of governments to respect, protect and promote the human rights of their peoples, both offline and online.

The next, and final, chapter, considers the prospects and challenges of big data and machine learning, in order to explore human rights in the age of artificial intelligence.

CHAPTER 8

HUMAN RIGHTS AND ARTIFICIAL INTELLIGENCE

1. INTRODUCTION

'Fuck the algorithm.' 'I am not my postcode.' London, August 2020. Thousands of placard waving students are marching in protest at their country's exam regulator, which used an algorithm to determine their final school year A level results.[1] I was following the story closely, having just spent two years, at the University of Otago, working on a project examining the legal implications of artificial intelligence.[2] New human rights issues were rapidly emerging in the fields of big data and machine learning. I saw similarities with my experiences of the Internet and human rights: technical communities of engineers, researchers and developers creating incredible tools, private sector investors, a civil society concerned about human rights interferences, and policymakers wondering how to respond. In this chapter, I briefly discuss some of these similarities, and consider their implications.

2. WHAT IS 'ARTIFICIAL INTELLIGENCE'?

'Artificial intelligence' (often known as AI) conjures up images of some kind of sentient machine or intelligent robot ('the singularity'). While there

---

1 J. PORTER, 'UK Ditches Exam Results Generated by Biased Algorithm after Student Protests', The Verge, 17.08.2020 <https://www.theverge.com/2020/8/17/21372045/uk-a-level-results-algorithm-biased-coronavirus-covid-19-pandemic-university-applications> accessed 17.09.2020.

2 The Artificial Intelligence and Law Project, funded by the New Zealand Law Foundation <http://www.cs.otago.ac.nz/research/ai/AI-Law/> accessed 17.09.2020. This chapter also draws on aspects of my project research, and my contribution to the privacy chapter in J. ZERILLI et al, *A Citizen's Guide to Artificial Intelligence*, MIT Press, Cambridge, MA 2021, pp. 93–106.

are a few very convincing 'puppets', like Sophia, the first robot to be granted citizenship,[3] this type of AI, known as general AI, is still a very long way off. According to David Kaye, who succeeded Frank La Rue as Special Rapporteur on Freedom of Opinion and Expression, 'artificial intelligence' is something of a misnomer, since it suggests 'that machines can operate according to the same concepts and rules as human intelligence. They cannot'.[4] The large gap between the scientific definitions and popular public perceptions of AI mean that there is 'no widely accepted definition of 'artificial intelligence'.[5]

For now, the focus is on the much narrower AI techniques. AI with very specific applications are being developed and deployed. The field of narrow AI is largely an extension of the statistical field of predictive analytics or mathematical predictive models, which has grown exponentially with the use of massive computing power to support its processes. There are a variety of predictive analytics and modelling methods, such as decision trees, neural networks and Bayesian models, which use algorithms (mathematical formulas that create outputs) trained on large amounts of data. 'Big data', in this context, is a term describing data that is large in volume, capable of being processed at speed, and which is diverse in its form or nature. Algorithms can use big data to generate all kinds of predictive results. These results are, in turn, used in a wide variety of new AI tools.

Whether you know it or not, you are, almost certainly, already using or training at least one of these AI tools, which are an increasingly significant part of daily life: they are contained in voice-operated Internet search functions, customer service chatbots, targeted online advertising, navigation assistance mapping services, and self-driving cars, to name just a few.[6] Tools in homes, cars, public CCTV cameras and many other places are 'learning' from data collected in your everyday interactions, and those of millions of other people, in order to respond faster and with

---

3 See Hanson Robotics, 'Sophia' <https://www.hansonrobotics.com/sophia/> accessed 07.03.2021.

4 D. KAYE, 'Report of the Special Rapporteur to the General Assembly on AI and its Impact on Freedom of Opinion and Expression', United Nations, A/73/348, 29.08.2018, p. 3 <https://www.ohchr.org/EN/Issues/FreedomOpinion/Pages/ReportGA73.aspx> accessed 07.03.2021.

5 House of Lords Select Committee on Artificial Intelligence, 'AI in the UK: Ready, Willing and Able?', 2018, HL Paper 100, para. 9 <https://publications.parliament.uk/pa/ld201719/ldselect/ldai/100/10002.htm> accessed 07.03.2021.

6 D. KAYE, above n. 4, pp. 3–6.

more accuracy. Kaye neatly summarises the machine-human interface in this way:[7]

> In all circumstances, humans play a critical role in designing and disseminating AI systems, defining the objectives of an AI application and, depending on the type of application, selecting and labelling datasets and classifying outputs. Humans always determine the application and use of AI outputs, including the extent to which they complement or replace human decision-making.

Despite AI's machine-like image, then, it is in fact humans at the centre of all stages of the design, deployment and implementation of narrow AI. When Covid-19 caused A level exams to be cancelled in the United Kingdom, it was, therefore, people at the Office of Qualification and Examinations Regulation (Ofqual) who, with good intentions, decided to use an algorithmic process to help fairly determine students' final results. Ofqual determined the results using two sources: the ranking of students within schools, and their schools' historical results. The outcome was national results that, overall, largely mirrored those of the previous year, but which also caused significant unfairness in many individual cases because there was no direct connection between a student's past achievement and their allocated predicted grade.[8]

In England, for example, while there was an overall increase in the level of high grades nationally, nearly 40 per cent of grades were lower than teacher predictions. Many students lost the university places they had been offered. In addition, students at independent, private schools saw the biggest increases in grades, while students at state-run schools saw the biggest decreases: the algorithm results rewarded poorly performing students in wealthy schools and penalised high-performing students in poorer schools.[9] The resulting outrage caused Ofqual's chief executive to resign, and the results to be ditched in favour of alternative, teacher-led assessments. Artificial? Yes: Intelligent? No.

A combination of the rapidly increasing availability of AI tools, and their ease of use in areas where demand for automation of simple business

---

[7] ibid., p. 4.

[8] S. COUGHLAN, 'Why did the A-level Algorithm say No?', BBC News, 14.08.2020 <https://www.bbc.com/news/education-53787203> accessed 01.09.2020.

[9] S. COUGHLAN, K. SELLGREN and J. BURNS, 'A-levels: Anger over "unfair" results this year', BBC News, 13.08.2020 <https://www.bbc.com/news/education-53759832> accessed 02.09.2020.

rules is high, has seen a surge in use of AI tools at the same time as there are significant concerns about their immediate, medium- and long-term implications. The overall picture is changing rapidly and, as it does, more human rights issues are emerging.

3. AI TOOLS AND HUMAN RIGHTS

Research on the benefits and opportunities posed by AI has ballooned in the last three years.[10] National research institutes, private consortiums and international collaborations have formed at a rapid pace, and in an environment where there is little direct regulation. As with Covid-19 digital proximity tracing apps, as quickly as AI tools are developed and deployed, so too are human rights concerns growing. By way of introduction, the next section looks at just a few of these: bias and discrimination, transparency and the right to due process, and the right to privacy.

3.1. ALGORITHMIC BIAS AND DISCRIMINATION

In theory, the use of mathematical formulas, rather than us fallible humans, should increase our chances of fair treatment: the same rules are applied to everyone equally, all of us judged without bias. In fact, as Cathy O'Neil famously describes, in her powerful book *Weapons of Math Destruction*, this is not true: there are many instances of biased and unfair automated systems in healthcare, criminal justice, education and finance. Worse still, they can reinforce discrimination.[11] Bias in algorithmic processes can have a variety of unintended effects, such as filter bubbles in social media, or algorithmic echo chambers.[12]

Algorithmic bias can arise from errors and biases in training data sets. A machine learning tool that disproportionately classifies African

---

10 See, e.g. F. RASO et al, 'Artificial Intelligence and Human Rights: Opportunities and Risks', Research Publication No. 2018-6, Berkman Klein Center for Internet and Society, Harvard University, 25.09.2018 <https://cyber.harvard.edu/publication/2018/artificial-intelligence-human-rights> accessed 31.08.2020.

11 C. O'NEIL, *Weapons of Math Destruction: How Big Data Increases Inequality and Threatens Democracy*, Crown Random House, New York 2016.

12 Committee of Experts on Internet Intermediaries (MSI-NET), 'Algorithms and Human Rights: Study on the Human Rights Dimensions of Automated Data Processing Techniques and Possible Regulatory Implications', Council of Europe study DGI (2017) 12, p. 11.

American men as posing a greater risk of recidivism, for example, was probably trained on a set of data reflecting racial prejudice inherent in discriminatory patterns of policing.[13] In order to avoid bias, an algorithm must have a definition of fairness, but there are human rights problems with some of the technical definitions of fairness. For example, Corbett-Davies and Goel concluded, in 2018, that none of the mathematically popular definitions of fairness – anti-classification, classification parity and calibration – satisfied the requirements of non-discrimination and equitable treatment in relation to similarly situated people.[14] The search for definitions of fairness for use in AI remains elusive and contested and, without technical experts helping, most of us would not understand the issue.

Closely connected to algorithmic bias is algorithmic discrimination. If trained on a narrow set of cultural or social contexts, online content moderation algorithms might perpetuate bias by being unable to take into account cultural, social or political contexts or languages. There have been criticisms, for example, of the autocomplete function in Google's search engine for producing racist results,[15] and of algorithmically driven advertisements for having discriminatory effects.[16]

The fallacy of the impartial mathematical formula is also apparent when it comes to gender. Perhaps it should come as no surprise, given the lack of women in the AI development workforce, to find that AI tools are not 'gender neutral'. In fact, their gendered nature has been revealed in numerous ways, from how women are represented in AI tools (such as sexualised female service robots, and the predominant use of female voices in apps and chat tools), to the services offered to women by algorithms designed to be 'gender blind'. Soon after launching a new credit card in 2019, for example, Apple ran into problems when heterosexual married

---

13 See, e.g. J. LARSEN et al, 'How We Analysed the COMPAS Recidivism Algorithm', ProPublica, 23.05.2016 <www.propublica.org> accessed 12.09.2020; K. LUM and W. ISAAC, 'To Predict and Serve? (2016) 13 (5) *Significance* 14.

14 S. CORBETT-DAVIES and S. GOEL, 'The Measure and Mismeasure of Fairness: A Critical Review of Fair Machine Learning', v.2, arXiv.org, 14.08.2018 <https://arxiv.org/abs/1808.00023> accessed 02.09.2020.

15 P. MARTINEAU, 'YouTube's Search Suggests Racist Autocompletes', The Outline, 13.05.2018 <https://theoutline.com/post/4536/youtube-s-search-autofill-suggests-racist-results> accessed 16.03.2021.

16 See, e.g. L. SWEENEY, 'Discrimination in Online Ad Delivery', Data Privacy Lab, Harvard University, 28.01.2013 <https://dataprivacylab.org/projects/onlineads/1071-1.pdf> accessed 17.09.2020; F. PASQUALE, *The Black Box Society: the Secret Algorithms that Control Money and Information*, Harvard University Press, Cambridge, MA 2014.

customers noticed that it offered smaller lines of credit to female spouses than it did to males.[17] Apple and card issuer Goldman Sachs issued statements denying discrimination, saying that the determinations were made on an individual, not family, basis, and not on the basis of gender.[18] Commentators pointed out that, while the discrimination may not have been intentional, there was already clear evidence of the harmful consequences of failing to take gender and other protected characteristics into account.[19]

This hidden bias in AI tools has also been revealed in facial recognition systems sold by large tech companies, giving rise to serious concerns about algorithmic discrimination. Joy Buolamwini, founder of the Algorithmic Justice League, published research showing that facial recognition systems on IBM, Microsoft and Face++ were worse at recognising women's faces compared to men's. Dark-skinned females were the most frequently misclassified group (having an error rate of up to 34.7 per cent, compared to an error rate of up to just 0.8 per cent for white males).[20] Both Microsoft and IBM have upgraded their data sets as a result.[21]

In follow-up research, Buolamwini and co-researcher Raji found that Amazon's facial recognition tool, Rekognition, was also discriminatory: the software showed no errors identifying the gender of lighter-skinned males, but mistook lighter-skinned women for men 19 per cent of the time, and mistook darker-skinned females for males 34 per cent of the time.[22]

---

17 W. KNIGHT, 'The Apple Card Didn't "See" Gender and That's the Problem', Wired, 19.11.2019 <https://www.wired.com/story/the-apple-card-didnt-see-genderand-thats-the-problem/> accessed 17.09.2020.

18 I. A. HAMILTON, 'Goldman Sachs will Let People Appeal their Apple Credit Card Limit after Allegations of Sexist Algorithms,' Business Insider Australia, 12.11.2019 <https://www.businessinsider.com.au/goldman-sachs-apple-card-sexism-response-2019-11?r=US&IR=T> accessed 17.09.2020.

19 K. COX, 'NY Regulators Investigating Apple after Viral Complaint of Sexism', Ars Technica, 12.11.2019 <https://arstechnica.com/tech-policy/2019/11/ny-regulators-investigating-apple-card-after-viral-complaint-of-sexism/> accessed 17.09.2020.

20 J. BUOLAMWINI and T. GERBU, 'Gender Shades: Intersectional Accuracy Disparities in Commercial Gender Recognition' (2018) *Proceedings of Machine Learning Research* 81:1–15, Conference on Fairness, Accountability and Transparency <http://gendershades.org/> accessed 15.09.2020.

21 J. VINCENT, 'Gender and Racial Bias found in Amazon's Facial Recognition Technology (Again)', The Verge, 25.01.2019 <https://www.theverge.com/2019/1/25/18197137/amazon-rekognition-facial-recognition-bias-race-gender> accessed 17.09.2020.

22 I. D. RAJI and J. BUOLAMWINI, 'Actionable Auditing: Investigating the Impact of Publicly Naming Biased Performance Results of Commercial AI Products'

Amazon defended its technology, challenging the research findings, but the pair stood firm, saying that the technology, which is sold to law enforcement agencies, exhibited gender and racial bias, and warning that '[u]nchecked, widely deployed facial identification technology can lead to mass surveillance and unprecedented risks to civil liberties'.[23] The researchers called for a halt to the use of facial recognition systems in policing, and for Amazon to submit their AI systems to the US National Institute of Standards and Technology for the latest rounds of facial recognition evaluations.

The recent heinous death of George Floyd led to global condemnation of racial inequality and police brutality. In the wake of related 'Black Lives Matter' protests and widespread public concerns, IBM announced that it was leaving the facial recognition business.[24] Amazon announced that it was placing a one-year moratorium on the sale of its facial recognition system to law enforcement agencies until there was stronger regulation of such technologies.[25] While this move was welcomed by some, others considered it meaningless without knowing the steps being taken during the moratorium to address the real causes of algorithmic bias, and the consequent dangers of facial recognition technologies in the hands of law enforcement agencies.[26]

In addition to race and gender bias, research has revealed unfair discriminatory effects on economic, health and social security rights from AI tools. For example, in *Automating Inequality*, Virginia Eubanks set out a powerful in-depth analysis of data-based discrimination, outlining the

---

(2019) Association for the Advancement of Artificial Intelligence <https://www.aies-conference.com/2019/wp-content/uploads/2019/01/AIES-19_paper_223.pdf> accessed 17.09.2020.

23 J. BUOLAMWINI, 'Response: Racial and Gender Bias in Amazon Rekognition – Commercial Systems for Analyzing Faces', Medium, 25.01.2019 <https://medium.com/@Joy.Buolamwini/response-racial-and-gender-bias-in-amazon-rekognition-commercial-ai-system-for-analyzing-faces-a289222eeced> accessed 03.09.2020.

24 L. HIRSCH, 'IBM Gets out of Facial Recognition Business, Calls on Congress to Advance Policies Tackling Racial Injustice', CNBC News, 08.06.2020 <https://www.cnbc.com/2020/06/08/ibm-gets-out-of-facial-recognition-business-calls-on-congress-to-advance-policies-tackling-racial-injustice.html > accessed 07.03.2021.

25 K. PAUL, 'Amazon to Ban Police Facial Recognition Software for a Year', *The Guardian*, 11.06.2020 <https://www.theguardian.com/technology/2020/jun/10/amazon-rekognition-software-police-black-lives-matter> accessed 03.09.2020.

26 Privacy International, 'Why Amazon's Temporary Ban of Police Use of Facial Recognition is not Enough', 11.06.2020 <https://privacyinternational.org/news-analysis/3896/why-amazons-temporary-ban-police-use-facial-recognition-not-enough> accessed 14.09.2020.

effects of data mining, policy algorithms and other predictive tools on poor and working-class people.[27] Eubanks shows how decision-making systems built by humans in areas such as health care, social security and child welfare are entrenching a modern 'digital poorhouse', which needs to be dismantled.[28]

3.2. TRANSPARENCY AND DUE PROCESS

The Ofqual example above is just one of many that highlights how AI tools differ from the Internet and other information communication technologies, being more complex and less transparent.[29] Unlike traditional statistical tools to assist decision-making, machine and deep learning systems are essentially 'black boxes': the systems are so complex that knowing how results have been produced may be impossible, both for developers and users. In addition, the rules protecting the commercially sensitive information used to develop AI tools, such as intellectual property laws, exacerbate this lack of transparency, making it difficult, if not impossible, to challenge decisions that have been made using such tools. This has proved to be an especially difficult problem in the criminal justice system.

The uses of predictive algorithms in the criminal justice system are very diverse, ranging from policing (predicting crimes and perpetrator or victim identities) to crime detection, prosecution decisions, and post-conviction decisions on sentencing and parole. While the use of predictive tools in criminal justice is not new, the use of algorithm-based predictive models raises new concerns about the data driving the predictive tools, and its potential to reinforce existing policing practices without transparency or due process. In 2016, for example, Eric Loomis unsuccessfully challenged the use of the Correctional Offender Management Profiling for Alternate Sanctions (COMPAS) algorithm to aid determination of his sentence by a Wisconsin judge.[30] The company that developed the tool refused to provide details of the model, citing this as a trade secret, with the result that

---

27 V. EUBANKS, *Automating Inequality: How High-Tech Tools Profile, Police and Punish the Poor*, Picador/St Martin's Press, New York 2018.

28 ibid., p. 211.

29 For a general overview, see C. GAVAGHAN, J. MCLAURIN, A. KNOTT, J. ZERILLI and J. LIDDICOAT, *Government Use of Artificial Intelligence in New Zealand*, University of Otago and New Zealand Law Foundation, Wellington 2020, pp. 30–48.

30 *Wisconsin v Loomis* 881 NW 2d 749 (Wis. 2016).

Mr Loomis could not examine how COMPAS created a risk score. Although the court expressed concerns about the use of COMPAS in sentencing decisions, it found that Mr Loomis could not review or challenge how the algorithm calculated risk. It did find, however, that he could still seek review of the risk scores that the algorithm generated. Organisations such as ProPublica have criticised the COMPAS tool, saying that it incorrectly assesses black defendants as having a higher risk of reoffending compared to white defendants and white defendants were more likely to be wrongly assessed as being a low risk compared to black defendants.[31]

Automated AI systems also differ from the Internet because they are designed to learn: to identify problems and come up with solutions. Results can vary, depending on how these systems are supervised, and how they are taught to learn by their human developers: for example, to know what errors are, and how to identify them. Knowing exactly how an AI tool has produced results can be so complicated that new neural networks and AI explanation tools have been developed to help explain their outputs. Such explanation tools are models trained to understand how one automated machine learning process produced its results by programming another one to reproduce its performance,[32] such as new, open source fairness audits.[33] The University of Chicago's Aequitas, for example, provides an open-source toolkit for machine learning developers, policymakers and data analysts to self-audit their AI tools for bias.[34] Another, AI Fairness 360, enables users to 'examine, report and mitigate discrimination and bias in machine learning models'.[35]

Transparency and due process includes the right to challenge or review decisions, to hold the person making the decision accountable. But what is the appropriate level of accountability of the person who makes a decision while relying on information produced by an AI tool? Following the liability chain can become a bit like the nursery rhyme about the plight of the old

---

31 J. LARSEN, S. MATTU, L. KIRCHNER and J. ANGWIN, 'How we Analysed the COMPAS Recidivism Algorithm', ProPublica, 23.05.2016 <https://www.propublica.org/article/how-we-analyzed-the-compas-recidivism-algorithm> accessed 14.12.2020.

32 L. EDWARDS and M. VEALE, 'Slave to the Algorithm? Why a "Right to an Explanation" is Probably Not the Remedy You Are Looking For', *Duke Law and Technology Law Review* (2017) Vol. 16:1, 18.

33 N. MEHRABI et al, 'A Survey on Bias and Machine Learning', 17.09.2019, arXiv.org <https://arvix.org/abs/1908.09635> accessed 30.08.2020.

34 Center for Data Science and Public Policy, University of Chicago, 'Aequitas' <http://www.datasciencepublicpolicy.org/projects/aequitas/> accessed 14.09.2020.

35 IBM Trusted Research AI, 'AI Fairness 360' <https://aif360.mybluemix.net/> accessed 14.09.2020.

lady who swallowed a fly, then swallowed a spider to catch the fly, then a bird to catch the spider, a cat to catch the bird, and so on, ad infinitum. The answer may depend on whether the AI tool replaces or simply augments a human decision maker. In some situations, it might be unclear who is accountable: the algorithm developer, the person who provided data that programmed the algorithm, the company using it, or the third party that placed the algorithm within a product that has caused harm.[36]

3.3. PRIVACY AND DATA PROTECTION

Machine learning tools rely on the collection and use of data, including personal information. A new privacy concern is the amount of 'ambient' data collection taking place via devices (such as consumer products fitted with sensors) that are in close proximity to us. Anonymised data sets obtained from this kind of ambient data collection are offered for sale by data brokers to AI developers, but there are significant concerns about risks of re-identification and the security of techniques for anonymity. A French study in 2015, for example, found that mobile phone users within an anonymised data set could be re-identified with 75 per cent probability by using machine learning methods and data from two smartphone apps, with probability of re-identification rising to 95 per cent if four apps were used.[37]

AI tools can be used to categorise and rank people, often without their consent, affecting their entitlements to insurance, credit or social services. The lack of consent, and the blurring of lines between personal and non-personal information (a fundamental distinction in data protection law) are other concerns. The creation of new data sets can also make it difficult to know where your personal information is going and how it is being used. Using data in contexts far removed from its origins also poses a greater risk that AI tools will produce errors.[38]

New forms of privacy rights are emerging in response to the dangers posed by big data analytics. International human rights law recognises

---

36 Committee of Experts on Internet Intermediaries, above n. 12, p. 12.

37 J. P. ACHARA et al, 'On the Unicity of Smartphone Applications' 14th ACM Workshop on Privacy in the Electronic Society, October 2015, pp. 27–36, arXiv.org <https://arxiv.org/pdf/1507.07851v2.pdf>.

38 Article 19 & Privacy International, *Privacy and Freedom of Expression in the Age of Artificial Intelligence* (Report), April 2018 <https://www.article19.org/resources/privacy-freedom-expression-age-artificial-intelligence/> accessed 07.03.2021.

and protects certain groups, such as indigenous peoples or unions, and characteristics, such as race, sex or political belief. Algorithmic processes might result in the creation of new groups of people not based on these protected characteristics. Brent Mittelstadt, for example, argues that data analytics can give rise to new types of algorithmically assembled groups, which do not necessarily align with classes or attributes that are already protected by human rights law, creating a need to move from individual to group privacy concepts and rights. New types of groups that might assert privacy rights, Mittelstadt suggests, include collectives (unions or patient advocacy groups), ascriptive groups (with a shared characteristic such as an ethnic group), and ad hoc groups (such as time or purpose groups like market segments or profile groups).[39]

In summary, as the field of narrow AI rapidly develops so too has a myriad of human rights issues emerged. This, in turn, raises the question of how, if at all, to regulate the development and deployment of AI tools.

4. REGULATORY APPROACHES

Many of the regulatory approaches to the Internet described in Chapter 5 are available for the regulation of AI: hands-off permissionless innovation, the precautionary principle, technological determinism (the idea there is no good or bad technology, so leave it to technologists), and the dividend distribution approach (intervention to ensure equitable distribution of benefits). However, there are some key differences in the starting points for AI, compared to the Internet, and these are relevant when weighing up regulatory options.

Like the Internet, AI started off being developed largely in closed research programmes, many of which are still co-funded by governments as they race to compete with each other. But, unlike the Internet, which was designed for sharing – to be an ever-expanding, open, free network – AI is not, for the most part, being designed as a global public resource that will be openly available to all. While there are patches of open AI, such as Google's OpenAI platform,[40] these are small in proportion to the vast amount of AI development.

---

39 B. MITTELSTADT, 'From Individual Privacy to Group Privacy in Big Data Analytics' (2017) *Philosophy and Technology*, 30, 475–94 <https://link.springer.com/article/10.1007/s13347-017-0253-7> accessed 07.03.2021.

40 Google, OpenAI initiative <www.openai.com> accessed 07.03.2021.

AI is also framed quite differently in human rights discourse. The Internet was positioned as the very embodiment of human rights (an inspiring, ultimate freedom), empowering users in a decentralised network. The entry points for the Internet in the international human rights system were freedom of expression, free flow of information, freedom of association, Internet access, and the right to privacy. There was little focus on Internet-related harms, although there were concerns about interferences with the Internet, including harmful content.

The starting point for AI and human rights is quite different. There is a sense of fear rather than freedom; a clear realisation of how harmful AI can be.[41] The entry points for international human rights reflect this: harms from bias and discrimination, lack of due process and transparency, and concerns for privacy. Exacerbating this is another factor: AI tools may replace or augment human decision-making or performance, over which there are already well-established human rights rules. Specific applications of AI tools for such purposes are causing alarm, such as the dangerous implications of autonomous lethal weapons (killer robots and drones) that could select targets and apply force without proper human control.[42] The Campaign to Stop Killer Robots, for example, has called for these to be prohibited under the Convention on Certain Conventional Weapons, to ensure that meaningful human control remains over autonomous weapons systems.[43]

In the direction of permissionless innovation for AI, are those favouring no rules or other market influences that might interfere with competition to be the safest, easiest or cheapest place for AI investment. Governments fear being left behind, or losing their position through 'first mover disadvantage', where being the first to regulate results in being left behind or missing out on a development that will make their country great, greater or great again. There can also be difficulties in working out regulatory approaches towards

---

41 M. GALVIN, 'Human Rights in the Age of Social, Media, Big Data and AI', Symposium Summary, National Academy of Sciences Engineering and Medicine, 23.09.2019 <https://www.nationalacademies.org/news/2019/09/human-rights-in-age-of-social-media-big-data-and-ai> accessed 16.03.2021.

42 R. A. RAHIM, 'The Weaponisation of AI: An Existential Threat to Human Rights and Dignity' in *Global Information Society Watch 2019*, Association for Progressive Communications, Article 19 and Sida, pp. 42–46 <https://www.giswatch.org/2019-artificial-intelligence-human-rights-social-justice-and-development> accessed 07.03.2021; Human Rights Watch, 'Statement to the CCW Consultation on Lethal Autonomous Weapons Systems', 28.06.2019 <https://www.hrw.org/news/2019/06/28/statement-ccw-consultation-lethal-autonomous-weapons-systems> accessed 17.09.2020.

43 Campaign to Stop Killer Robots <https://www.stopkillerrobots.org> accessed 18.09.2020.

technologies that are still under development, for example will regulations for self-driving cars today be far-sighted, or outdated before they come into force?

But pressure is growing for pre-emptive rules, as AI technology moves so quickly that retrospective regulation risks more harm than doing nothing. In the precautionary principle direction are many academics and civil society groups. 2018, for instance, was a volatile year in the world of AI: from social media platforms inciting racial hatred and ethnic cleansing in Myanmar, to multiple worker uprisings over Amazon's conditions in algorithmically managed warehouses, to Cambridge Analytica using AI tools to manipulate the results of an election. In response, groups such as the AI Now Institute called for basic precautionary safeguards of responsibility, liability and due process.[44] An increasing number of corporations have also sought reassurances that their significant investments in research and development will be protected when they go to market, making some of them more favourably disposed to regulatory certainty now, or soon, rather than later, or not at all.

Others, however, are calling for tougher policy settings for businesses. For example, Alan Dignam has suggested requiring corporations to act in the public interest if they want to set AI policy; mandating new corporate governance principles, such as prioritising use of AI for dangerous or difficult human tasks; requiring corporations to appoint public interest board members; or setting standards for responsibilities and risk, if existing rules on liability are inadequate. Dignam has pointed out that corporate governance models in owner- or founder-operated or controlled companies are especially troubling, since many do not meet the basic standards for corporate governance in publicly listed companies, such as those set by the British Standards Institution.[45] Accordingly, fundamental reform of corporate governance among the small number of listed companies developing new technologies is favoured, even if simply to apply existing standards.

New governance ideas have also emerged, focussing, for example, on the roles and responsibilities of organisations entrusted with data sets, or with overseeing machine learning and other automated algorithmic processes. Data governance is one way to control a key input for AI tools.

---

44 AI Now Institute, 'Annual Report', New York, 2018 <https://ainowinstitute.org/reports.html> accessed 07.03.2021.

45 A. DIGNAM, 'Artificial Intelligence: The Very Human Dangers of Dysfunctional Design and Autocratic Corporate Governance', Queen Mary University of London School of Law Legal Studies Research Paper, No. 314/2019.

Proposals include information fiduciaries, civic data trusts, and data trusts created in bottom-up processes where citizens choose to pool their data with a trust that would champion an economic or social cause of their choosing.[46] In this direction, new practical accountability tools, such as algorithmic impact assessments, have developed. In Canada, the use of algorithmic impact assessments has been mandated in government procurement practices,[47] while the Council of Europe's Commissioner for Human Rights has recommended steps to protect human rights in the development and deployment of AI tools.[48]

Alongside data governance sits AI governance, with some calling for a radical rethink of AI governance if the exacerbation of existing problems is to be avoided. Gurumurthy and Chami, for example, argue that none of the four main AI governance models (human rights, the future of work, the public sphere, and weaponising of AI technologies) are adequate to harness the potential of AI for development.[49]

While the regulatory approach to AI is still largely at the permissionless innovation end of the spectrum, there are signs of change. The research of Buolamwini and others is leading to an increased focus on precautionary regulation, to prevent and combat harms from the use of AI tools. The city of San Francisco, for example, has already banned facial recognition software, prohibiting its use by city agencies such as law enforcement or the transport authority.[50]

Perhaps the strongest approach has been in the European Union. In 2016, the EU enacted a new General Data Protection Regulation (GDPR). The GDPR contains a new general right, in Article 22, for a person '… not to be subject to a decision based solely on automatic

---

[46] P. DAWSON and G. ABUHAMAD, 'Towards Data Governance that Empowers the Public' in *Global Information Society Watch 2019*, Association for Progressive Communications, Article 19 and Sida, pp. 14–19 <https://www.giswatch.org> accessed 16.03.2021.

[47] Government of Canada, 'Directive on Automated Decision-Making' and 'Algorithmic Impact Assessment', 02.05.2019 <https://www.tbs-sct.gc.ca/pol/doc-eng.aspx?id=32592> accessed 13.09.2020.

[48] Commissioner for Human Rights, Council of Europe, 'Unboxing Artificial Intelligence: 10 Steps to Protect Human Rights', May 2019 <https://www.coe.int/en/web/commissioner/-/unboxing-artificial-intelligence-10-steps-to-protect-human-rights> accessed 07.03.2021.

[49] See, e.g. A. GURUMURTHY and N. CHAMI, 'The Wicked Problem of AI Governance' in *Artificial Intelligence in India, Vol. 2*, IT For Change and Friedrich-Ebert-Stiftung, New Delhi 2019.

[50] D. LEE, 'San Francisco is First US City to Ban Facial Recognition', BBC News, 14.05.2019 <https://www.bbc.com/news/technology-48276660> accessed 03.09.2020.

processing, including profiling, which produces legal effects concerning him or her or similarly significantly affects him or her'.[51] The new right does have some exceptions, but requires the data controller to implement 'suitable measures to safeguard the data subject's rights and freedoms and legitimate interests'. As a minimum, individuals must have 'the right to obtain human intervention' and the right 'to express his or her point of view and to contest the decision'.[52] Articles 13 to 15 of the GDPR also provide rights to 'meaningful information about the logic involved' in automated decision-making, which some argue is akin to the right to an explanation.[53] Others disagree strongly, saying that there is no right to a meaningful explanation in the GPDR,[54] while others suggest returning to the plain text and adopting a more purposive and functional approach, to enable a data subject to exercise their rights under the GDPR and human rights law.[55]

Finally, there have been calls for expansion of existing human rights to respond to new kinds of human rights violations, and to provide the necessary remedies. For example, Sandra Wachter and Brent Mittelstadt have argued for a new right to reasonable inferences, arguing that such a right is needed, given that individuals have little control or oversight over how their personal information is used by AI tools, which may make counter-intuitive inferences or adverse predictions about their behaviours, preferences or private lives.[56]

In summary, we are witnessing the emergence of a new human rights discourse in response to new AI tools. There are arguments for extension of existing rights, and for evolution of new rights and new remedies for new types of human rights violation. However, while proposals for regulation continued to develop, in the absence of a clear direction, a new phenomenon arose: the proposal of 'ethics' as a policy option.

---

51 EU General Data Protection Regulation 2016, Article 22 OJ L 119, 4.5.2016, p. 46.

52 ibid., Article 22(3).

53 B. GOODMAN and S. FLAXMAN, 'European Union Regulations on Algorithmic Decision-making and a "Right to Explanation"' (2016) ICML Workshop on Human Interpretability in Machine Learning, arXiv:1606.08813 (v3) <https://arxiv.org/abs/1606.08813> accessed 07.03.2021; (2017) 38 *AI Magazine* 50.

54 S. WACHTER, B. MITTELSTADT and L. FLORIDI, 'Why a Right to Automated Decision-making does not Exist in the General Data Protection Regulation' (2017) *International Data Privacy Law*, Vol. 7, No. 2, 76–99.

55 A. SELBST and J. POWLES, 'Meaningful Information and the Right to Explanation', *International Data Privacy Law*, Vol. 7, No. 4, 233–42.

56 S. WACHTER and B. MITTELSTADT, 'A Right to Reasonable Inferences: Rethinking Data Protection Law in the Age of Big Data and AI', *Columbia Business Law Review* 2019 (2).

5. ETHICS AND AI

In the era of communication rights, civil society groups reached for human rights as a way to navigate tensions between the basic operating principles and Protocols of the Internet and other forms of governance; to assert their freedoms, resist government control, and combat the weak legal controls over the private sector which enabled corporations to act with impunity. The technical community developed agreed Internet Protocols through open processes, and with underlying values such as rough consensus and running code.

Unlike Internet Protocols, however, there is no alternative set of standards or 'legal' system in the technical field of AI. There is no group of AI agencies that oversee technical coordination of network systems and protocols. On the contrary, one significant concern about the field of AI is the *lack* of agreed standards among the technical community, whether on definitions of fairness, error reporting or decision explanation.

Perhaps partially because of this, ethics has emerged as another possible standards framework. For example, concerns about the lack of ethical standards led the Institute of Electrical and Electronics Engineers to issue a call for comments on a new initiative, the 'Ethics Certification Program for Autonomous and Intelligent Systems', which has the goal of generating trust marks to show that an AI system is transparent, accountable, and fair.[57]

Drawing from the field of philosophy, ethics can help answer difficult questions in the field of AI, such as whether there are there situations where an automated tool should *never* be used (such as in a self-driving car, where human life is in immediate danger) or, conversely, whether there might be situations where AI *must* be used (such as where an AI tool performs better at reading cancer screening images than a doctor).[58] Ethics can also assist with proper approaches to publicising and reporting errors in AI tools, so that tools can be updated, changed or rendered obsolete when appropriate.

---

57 Institute of Electrical and Electronics Engineers, 'Ethics Certification Program for Autonomous and Intelligent Systems' <https://standards.ieee.org/industry-connections/ecpais.html> accessed 19.09.2020.

58 A. M. FROOMKIN, I. KERR and J. PINEAU 'When AIs Outperform Doctors: Confronting the Challenges of a Tort-Induced Over-Reliance on Machine Learning' (2019) *Arizona Law Review*, Vol. 61: 33.

With echoes of the communications and Internet rights era, a plethora of ethical principles, statements and charters have been developed. Microsoft,[59] Google,[60] and IBM,[61] for example, have all released principles on ethical or responsible use of AI. Intergovernmental organisations have also got in on the act, such as the European Commission, with its 'ethical principles and democratic prerequisites' for AI, robotics and autonomous technology,[62] the OECD, with its expert group on AI in Society,[63] and the G20 group of countries, with principles for responsible stewardship of artificial intelligence.[64]

National initiatives have also appeared, such as Singapore's Advisory Council on Ethical Use of Artificial Intelligence and Data, and the UK's House of Lords Select Committee on Artificial Intelligence. In China, the Ministry of Science and Technology has issued a set of principles for next generation AI governance, pledging to develop responsible AI.[65]

By 2019, researchers had uncovered no fewer than 84 documents containing ethical principles or guidelines for AI, and 88 per cent were released after 2016.[66] But there is considerable scepticism, and serious concern, that behind the sudden appearance of ethical statements and charters is a desire to avoid or circumvent regulation, or to protect industry self-regulation. Ben Wagner, for example, has warned of 'ethics shopping' (with such an array to choose from, governments and corporations can

---

59 Microsoft, 'Microsoft AI Principles' <https://www.microsoft.com/en-us/ai/responsible-ai?activetab=pivot1%3aprimaryr6> accessed 19.09.2020.

60 Google, 'Artificial Intelligence at Google: Our Principles' <https://ai.google/principles> accessed 19.09.2020.

61 IBM Group, 'Everyday Ethics for Artificial Intelligence' <https://www.ibm.com/watson/assets/duo/pdf/everydayethics.pdf> accessed 19.09.2020.

62 European Group on Ethics in Science and New Technologies, 'Statement on Artificial Intelligence, Robotics and "Autonomous" Systems', European Commission, Brussels, 2018.

63 Organisation for Economic Co-operation and Development, 'Recommendations of the Council on Artificial Intelligence' OECD/LEGA/0049 <https://legalinstruments.oecd.org/en/instruments/OECD-LEGAL-0449> and <http://www.oecd.org/going-digital/ai/principles/> accessed 19.09.2020.

64 'G20 Ministerial Statement on Trade and Digital Economy', June 2019 <https://www.mofa.go.jp/files/000486596.pdf> accessed 19.09.2020.

65 X. BO, 'China Issues Principles of Next Generation AI Governance', Xinhua, 18.06.2019 <http://www.xinhuanet.com/english/2019-06/18/c_138152819.htmAI> accessed 19.09.2020.

66 A. JOBIN, M. IENCA and E. VAYENA, 'Artificial Intelligence: The Global Landscape of Ethics Guidelines', Health Ethics and Policy Lab Switzerland, 2019, pp. 3–5 <https://arxiv.org/ftp/arxiv/papers/1906/1906.11668.pdf> accessed 19.09.2020.

simply choose those principles which suit them best) and 'ethics washing' (the 'rinsing' of AI development through an ethical framework that has no real meaning, or which does not align with legal standards).[67]

Some ethical approaches could be linked to regulatory options. For example, should there be a requirement to maintain an AI tool so that it does not become out of date? What ethical duties should there be in relation to errors? Should companies be required to publicly report and correct errors, in much the same way as they report data breaches or publicise consumer product faults? A related question is whether to maintain or create new legal 'safe harbours' to support ethical practice, of the kind used to protect Internet intermediaries carrying traffic on the network, but to protect citizens, not developers. For example, if an AI tool produces a racist outcome, should the question of how it did so be irrelevant? Would this kind of legal liability create other risks, such as a reluctance to report errors? If so, would a better approach be to introduce validation flags and support ethical practice, so that an AI tool can be corrected or improved, rather than recalled? Conversely, are these really simply legal questions of liability and accountability, rather than ethical questions?

Whatever the answer, one result of this significant ethical focus is the engagement of another group of experts in the field of technology and human rights: philosophers and ethicists. Some, such as Brent Mittelstadt, have warned strongly against thinking that ethical standards developed in one field, such as health, can easily be transferred into the field of AI.[68] Others, working with technology and human rights experts, have proposed new human rights protections. Virginia Eubanks, for example, has argued for basic technology design principles to minimise harms to humans, suggesting a new digital Hippocratic oath for data scientists, systems engineers, hackers and officials.[69]

Technology workers are also taking action to uphold ethics and human rights. In June 2018, for example, engineers at Google forced the company not to renew Project Maven, a contract with the Pentagon to improve drone strike accuracy using AI. Thousands of employees also joined

[67] B. WAGNER, 'Ethics as an Escape from Regulation: From Ethics-washing to ethics-shopping?' in M. HILDEBRANDT (ed.), *Being Profiling. Cogitas ergo sum*, Amsterdam University Press, Amsterdam 2018, pp. 84–89.

[68] B. MITTELSTADT, 'AI Ethics: Too Principled to Fail?', Oxford Internet Institute <https://arxiv.org/abs/1906.06668v1> and the updated paper 'Principles Alone Cannot Guarantee Ethical AI' (2019) *Nature Machine Intelligence* 1, 501–07, 18.02.2020, accessed 14.12.2020.

[69] V. EUBANKS, above n. 27, pp. 212–13 and 217.

with international human rights groups such as Amnesty International to express concerns about Google's Project Dragonfly, which aimed to create a censored search engine for the Chinese market.[70] The success of their efforts inspired similar efforts at Microsoft, Amazon and Salesforce. In June 2020, in response to the killing of George Floyd, more than 1,600 Google workers petitioned the company to remove police forces from Gmail, and end other police contracts.[71] In the field of AI, a new social movement named #TechWontBuildIt has emerged, made up of architects, engineers, developers, system operators and other experts in the technology industry who are concerned about the ethical implications of their employers' activities.[72]

6. AI AND ONLINE CONTENT: THE CHRISTCHURCH CALL

While there are significant differences between the human rights implications of the Internet and AI, the technologies do intersect. For instance, David Kaye has cited three particular intersections that raise human rights concerns: online content display and personalisation, online content moderation and removal, and online profiling and targeted advertising.[73]

Global multi-stakeholder efforts at regulating algorithms that manipulate online content moderation took a new turn in 2019. On 15 March 2019, a white supremacist committed terrorist attacks on two mosques in my home town of Christchurch, New Zealand.[74] The terrorist

---

70 Google Employees Against Dragonfly, 'We Are Google Employees. Google Must Drop Dragonfly', 27.11.2018 <https://medium.com/@googlersagainstdragonfly/we-are-google-employees-google-must-drop-dragonfly-4c8a30c5e5eb> accessed 04.09.2020.

71 B. MENEGUS, '1,600+ Googlers Call on Company to Kick Cops off Gmail', Gizmodo, 23.06.2020 <https://www.gizmodo.com.au/2020/06/1600-googlers-call-on-company-to-kick-cops-off-gmail-end-all-other-police-contracts/> accessed 04.09.2020.

72 See, e.g. Science for the People <https://scienceforthepeople.org/no-tech-for-ice/> accessed 04.09.2020; Tech Workers Coalition <https://collectiveaction.tech/> accessed 04.09.2020; and D. MACMILLAN and E. DWOSKIN, 'The War Inside Palantir: Data-mining Firm's Ties to ICE Under Attack by Employees', *The Washington Post*, 23.08.2019 <https://www.washingtonpost.com/business/2019/08/22/war-inside-palantir-data-mining-firms-ties-ice-under-attack-by-employees/> accessed 14.12.2020.

73 D. KAYE, above n. 4, pp. 6–9.

74 This section is based on my more detailed analysis in J. LIDDICOAT, 'Algorithms and Social Media: A Need for Regulation to Control Harmful Content' in *Global Information Society Watch Artificial Intelligence: Human Rights, Social Justice and*

murdered 51 people, and injured many others, as they were worshipping peacefully, and live-streamed his actions on Facebook. The attack was the worst of its kind in New Zealand's history, prompting an emotional nationwide outpouring of solidarity with Muslim communities. Prime Minister Jacinda Ardern travelled immediately to embrace the Muslim communities affected, framing the attack as one perpetrated on all New Zealanders, refusing to say the attacker's name, and pledging to ban semi-automatic weapons of the kind used in the attack.

Footage of the attack was broadcast using Facebook's live-streaming service, and was viewed 4,000 times in the 27 minutes before Facebook removed it. Even within that very short space of time, the video was uploaded to 4chan, 8chan and other platforms. Within 24 hours, the video had spread widely, and 1.5 million copies had been removed. During this time, there had been one upload per second to YouTube alone.[75]

I was one of many people who inadvertently saw part of the video. I was following the news, having received messages from my family in Christchurch that they were in lockdown and did not know what was happening. Watching the newsfeeds on Twitter, a video image appeared in my Twitter newsfeed of a person taking guns out of the back of a car. The video automatically began playing (despite my autoplay option being deactivated). Realising what it was, I immediately stopped watching, and tweeted: 'Please don't retweet copies of the live-streamed footage of the #ChristchurchMosque shooting. Don't fuel the fires of hate and anger or glorify those who did this'.

Many others, including the prime minister, also saw part of the video inadvertently while following news of the events on Twitter or other platforms, as algorithms automatically shared copies of the video in newsfeeds. Both the live-streaming and sharing caused widespread public disgust and distress. There were demands that online platforms should prevent their algorithms from promoting the extreme content in newsfeeds, and should remove all copies of the video. The country's classification office ruled the video content illegal, making it a criminal offence to possess it.[76]

Development, Association for Progressive Communications, Article 19 and Sida, 2019, pp. 178–83 <https://www.giswatch.org/2019-artificial-intelligence-human-rights-social-justice-and-development> accessed 07.03.2021.

75 ibid.

76 D. SHANKS, 'Christchurch Mosque Attack Live Stream' Office of Film and Literature Classification, Ref: 900148.000,18.03.2019 and see also the Censor's decision in relation to the attacker's manifesto: D. SHANKS 'The Great Replacement' Office of

The global response to both the attack and the live-streaming led Ardern and French president Macron to issue the Christchurch Call. Just a few months before, Macron told the global IGF that he believed it was 'necessary to regulate' the Internet.[77] The Christchurch Call sought a relatively narrow investigation into the use of algorithms by social media platforms, in order to identify and interfere with terrorist and extremist online content. Ardern made it clear that her focus was on the harm of online terrorist extremist content, saying that the 'task here is to find ways to protect the freedom of the internet and its power to do good, while working together to find ways to end its use for terrorism'. She asked social media companies to 'assess how your algorithms funnel people to extremist content and make transparent that work'.[78]

The outcomes of the Christchurch Call included a set of voluntary commitments by governments and online service providers that were 'intended to address the issue of terrorist and violent extremist content online'.[79] Online service providers agreed, for example, to:

> Review the operation of algorithms and other processes that may drive users towards and/or amplify terrorist and violent extremist content to better understand possible intervention points and to implement changes where this occurs. This may include using algorithms and other processes to redirect users from such content or the promotion of credible, positive alternatives or counter-narratives.

In New Zealand, these developments were widely debated. Some commentators agreed that social media platforms should no longer be able to say that they were not publishers, when their own algorithms enabled and drove content sharing, while others said that this was simply a new take on the old debate that Internet service providers should not be liable

---

Film and Literature Classification, Ref: 1900149.000, 23.08.2019 <https://www.classificationoffice.govt.nz/news/featured-classification-decisions/the-great-replacement/> accessed 18.09.2020. Several people have been convicted of possessing the video material.

77 E. MACRON, IGF Opening Ceremony Speech, 12.11.2018 <https://www.intgovforum.org/multilingual/content/igf-2018-speech-by-french-president-emmanuel-macron> accessed 14.12.2020.

78 J. ARDERN, 'Christchurch Call Opening Statement', 16.05.2020 <https://www.beehive.govt.nz/speech/jacinda-ardern%E2%80%99s-christchurch-call-opening-statement 16 May 2019> accessed 14.12.2020.

79 Office of the Prime Minister, New Zealand Government, 'Christchurch Call to Eliminate Terrorist and Violent Online Content Adopted', Press Release 16.05.2019 <https://www.beehive.govt.nz/release/christchurch-call-eliminate-terrorist-and-violent-extremist-online-content-adopted> accessed 14.12.2020.

for content.[80] There were technical difficulties identifying 'copies', as small changes could be made to the video (such as editing to add material), making it difficult to clearly identify the relevant content. Concerns were raised about the collateral damage to legitimate and legal content on online platforms, such as news media coverage. Some members of the Muslim community wanted to see the video (for example to see if family members had survived), and some had, in fact, already watched it. There were concerns that prohibiting the video would drive it to the so-called Dark Web, thereby embedding the harm that the authorities sought to eliminate.

However, others pointed out that these arguments were fallacious, since algorithms were already being used to curate and feed content, and could therefore be redesigned. They asserted that there may be ways to interfere with 'recommender' algorithms to prevent the development of filter bubbles that channel users to extremist content. Others decried Facebook's failure to implement their own community standards, and their initial silence after the attack.[81] Another view was that algorithms feeding the objectionable video content to those who did not want to see it was an interference with their right to privacy (their right to be left alone, and to decide for themselves what they wished to view).

Global civil society groups, such as Article 19, welcomed the initiative but expressed reservations. Executive director Thomas Hughes noted that the live video feature of online platforms has also been used as a tool to enable documentation of human rights abuses and prosecution of those who commit crimes, and that the failure to define 'terrorism' and 'violent extremism' left the proposals open to abuse by some governments.[82] The joint civil society statement about the Christchurch Call also emphasised the need to connect the online strategies with the offline structural and societal causes of terrorism.[83]

David Kaye helpfully questioned what tools were available to protect online speech that benefitted from participatory democratic processes and

---

80 R. BROWN 'This is not the Internet You Promised Us', The Spin Off, 12.04.2019 <https://thespinoff.co.nz/partner/actionstation/12-04-2019/this-is-not-the-internet-you-promised-us/> accessed 14.12.2020.

81 T. MANHIRE 'Mark Zuckerberg, Four Days on, Your Silence is Deafening', The Spinoff, 19.05.2019 <https://thespinoff.co.nz/society/19-03-2019/mark-zuckerberg-four-days-on-your-silence-on-christchurch-is-deafening/> accessed 14.12.2020.

82 T. HUGHES, 'Article 19's Response to the Christchurch Call to Action', Article 19, 14.05.2019 <https://www.article19.org/resources/article-19s-response-to-the-christchurch-call-to-action/> accessed 14.12.2020.

83 'Civil Society Positions on Christchurch Call Pledge', available at <https://www.eff.org/files/2019/05/16/community_input_on_christchurch_call.pdf> accessed 14.12.2020.

upheld fundamental human rights.[84] Options, Kaye suggested, included forcing companies to address their 'democratic deficits' through radically better transparency, and the application of human rights standards to content moderation norms. Those suggestions seem to be echoed in some of the agreed actions in the Christchurch Call.

While it is still too early to tell whether the Call has been successful, I have noted several significant aspects already. One is the fact such a negotiation took place at all; events such as NETmundial, the 2016 summit held in the wake of the Snowden revelations, seemed a thing of the past. Another is the very specific agreement about algorithms as a regulatory target. This signals an important step change in the regulatory approaches to AI tools, and represents a new sophistication in efforts to regulate online content consistently with human rights standards.

As I watched the moving and powerful testimony of victims at the sentencing of the attacker, it occurred to me that the Muslim community of Christchurch had been able to counter the narrative of religious intolerance on the global stage, not through regulatory reform, but by the character of its community actions offline. As humans design, build and use new technologies, social, legal and other tensions inevitably arise between both the benefits and opportunities, and the threats and risks that they pose. Nowhere will this be more evident in the next ten years than in the emerging field of artificial intelligence. Compared to the Internet and human rights, the field of AI and human rights is developing much more quickly: there is little debate that human rights apply, and more concern about a wider range of harms. International human rights standards are providing a clear foundation for general and specific human rights analyses, responses and remedies. The struggle to respect and protect human rights in AI has led to new social movements, new regulatory approaches and new expressions of human rights.

---

84 D. KAYE, *Speech Police: The Global Struggle to Govern the Internet*, Columbia Global Reports, New York 2019, pp. 115–26.

CONCLUSION

1. INTRODUCTION

This book was never intended as a philosophical treatise on the theoretical meaning of law, or a technical history of the Internet. I had intended it to be, mainly, a historical jurisprudential story for those curious about how certain legal standards relating to the Internet and human rights developed in the international human rights system. Yet, as I wrote, another story emerged. My experiences of working with activists, policymakers, human rights defenders and technical experts over more than ten years revealed the power of ordinary people and communities of experts to achieve extraordinary things when they work together. I decided to explore what insights this might offer for the future of human rights in the digital age.

2. SUMMARY

I have attempted, among other things, to chart the rise of the term 'human rights online' from the concept of communication rights, to Internet rights, to human rights online, and human rights in the digital age. Like the development of any new concept, the process has been iterative, owing its progress to those struggling to articulate their changing world in the realities of daily life. To understand the development of human rights online, we began, in Chapter 1, with an examination of the Internet. We saw that, at its core, the Internet operates as a distributed, end-to-end, decentralised network focussed on empowering those at the edges of its architecture with no central point of control. The technical community designed the network and the systems supporting it so that data could travel freely, without discrimination. The Internet was designed to be shared, and the network infrastructure was freely given away. Fundamentally, the Internet still works today because everyone uses the same Protocols, which were developed collaboratively by a diverse, multi-stakeholder community to make it work for everyone.

The international human rights system, on the other hand, operates as a government-centric system in which governments have affirmed that human rights belong to everyone, everywhere; that states have the right to govern; and that governments have related duties to respect, protect and promote the human rights of their citizens. As the Internet evolved, tensions quickly emerged between various groups about matters such as regulation of content, Internet access, and network control. New initiatives, such as Internet governance, emerged in response to these tensions. Yet, by the end of 2010, when the Internet had been challenging fundamental ideas about human rights for more than twenty years, and Twitter was already four years old, the international human rights system had still not squarely confronted the implications of the Internet or social media.

Chapter 2 examined how the case that human rights mattered in the context of the Internet was made by activists, citizen journalists, women's human rights defenders, and others who began using the Internet to freely monitor and document human rights abuses, and to organise against interferences with their Internet access and use. New kinds of interferences were examined, such as restrictions on Internet access, content filtering and blocking, covert email surveillance, harassment and detention of bloggers, criminalising certain types of speech, and new, punitive laws. In the case of Egypt, a large-scale Internet shutdown led citizen journalists, bloggers, and other human rights activists to demand that Internet access be protected as a human right. Some, such as the Egyptian activist Alaa Abd El-Fattah, are still fighting for justice. The chapter concluded with a discussion of why conceptualising human rights violations in the context of the Internet proved to be surprisingly difficult for mainstream human rights advocates and organisations. With no single, clear definition of a human rights violation, the basic framework of the international human rights system seemed difficult to apply to how the Internet actually worked. The framework of defined human rights and freedoms, with governments designated as duty-bearers charged with responsibility to respect and protect the human rights of their peoples, was at odds with a network-based system with no single point of control and no single line of accountability.

To demonstrate these difficulties, Chapter 3 examined the space between theory and practice, exploring the messy reality of the emerging field of human rights online by looking more closely at the definition of a human rights violation. In the absence of a single definition in international law, I took a broad approach that defined a human rights violation as having three basic elements: (a) a legally recognised right with a correlating rights-holder and duty-bearer; (b) an interference with that right which results in harm; and (c) a legal remedy for that harm. By examining the application of this broad definition to some examples of Internet interference, I demonstrated how these conceptual difficulties arose, why there were calls for new rights such as the right to be forgotten, and why there were difficulties in identifying social media platforms and private companies as duty-bearers. I outlined how women's human rights defenders, such as Khadija Ismayilova and Anita Sarkeesian, reported cases and monitored new forms of violence against women, such as cyberstalking or image manipulation, advocating for recognition of violence against women online as a harm and a human rights violation.

In Chapter 3, the questions of remedies and accountability for human rights violations were examined. For human rights defenders, arguments about the definition of human rights violations online were ultimately a question about who was to be held accountable for these; a question that still poses difficulties today. For the Internet community, the question of accountability was answered by how the Internet was designed: with free flow of data and no single point of control. Different perspectives on the theoretical and definitional issues meant that promoting and protecting human rights in the context of the Internet was difficult, even problematic, and took time to understand.

Chapter 4 explored advocacy strategies that sought to respond to these deep conceptual debates about the Internet and human rights. Communication rights emerged as one way to frame international human rights and new media. Civil society groups and others advocating for communication rights created a new movement tied closely to Internet governance initiatives such as the World Summit on the Information Society (WSIS). By the mid-to-late 2000s, however, as both the volume and types of Internet interferences increased, the concept of 'communication rights' seemed inadequate to capture the full range of human rights violations that were occurring. Instead, the idea of Internet rights emerged.

A wide range of multi-stakeholder Charters of Internet rights and principles initiatives attempted to articulate, and call for recognition of, human rights in the context of the Internet, such as the right to Internet access, the right to be free from content filtering, freedom of association online, and the right to share content. The private sector increasingly engaged in these initiatives, moving into new human rights territory, since business and the private sector were not, traditionally, actors in the international human rights system; nor were they duty-bearers in the same way as governments.

Governments were also grappling with policy development and taking a variety of regulatory approaches: these included permissionless innovation, precautionary regulation to avoid harm, technological determinism, and equitable digital dividend distribution. New regulatory challenges were constantly emerging, such as online technologies' convergence with the telecommunications and broadcasting sectors. Some of these sectors fell within the ambit of existing regulators, and some, such as content control on the Internet, did not. The roles and objectives for policymakers were unclear and, with little experience in the Internet, most governments and intergovernmental organisations were not well placed to regulate, leaving them genuinely struggling to find the best policy approaches.

Chapter 5 outlined how new standards for human rights online began to emerge. From modest beginnings, the work of the Special Rapporteur on Freedom of Opinion and Expression came to have significant effects. By the end of 2012, a new human rights concept had emerged: the simple premise that the same human rights we have offline also apply online. In the space of just a few years, the discourse of human rights and the Internet had, therefore, moved from communication rights, via Internet rights, to human rights online, bringing the Internet into the heart of the international human rights system. Civil society advocacy strategies that demanded accountability for Internet-related human rights violations pushed into the UN Universal Periodic Review process, and began to appear in the wider work programme of the Human Rights Council, other treaty bodies, and the Commission on the Status of Women.

Following on from this focus on freedom of expression, Chapter 6 considered the right to privacy, outlining how revelations about mass Internet surveillance led the international human rights system, with the help of human rights and technical communities, to develop new concepts of privacy and new definitions of human rights violations. At the same time, new collaborations grew between human rights and Internet rights organisations and those working to navigate the conceptual challenges and tensions between the openness and freedom of the Internet and accountability for human rights violations. Through this case study, we saw confirmation of the conceptual move beyond Internet rights, and a more fundamental transformation from the concept of human rights online to human rights in the digital age. Discussion of new rights emerged, including rights to anonymity, and to use encryption. A new mandate was created: that of the Special Rapporteur on the Right to Privacy.

These developments also had significant implications for Internet governance and the technical community. By the end of 2016, the separate orbits of the Internet and human rights were coming closer together, with small but significant human rights influences on the technical operation of the Internet. The Internet Engineering Task Force (IETF), for example, established a Human Rights Protocol Considerations Research Group, chartered to research whether Internet Protocols and standards enabled or threatened human rights. This group took, as its starting point, the possibility that failing to define and take account of the human rights-enabling characteristics of the Internet in Protocol development could result in these characteristics being degraded. The IETF also issued new guidance on privacy, and a new Request for Comments (RFC) relating to content filtering. The ICANN began working on a new by-law on human rights that would ultimately be relevant to its coordination of the global domain name system.

Chapter 7 examined the challenges of Covid-19 and argued that, far from being dismissed, human rights have instead been at the forefront of technology-related public health responses to the global pandemic. Three types of digital proximity contact tracing technologies, and the human rights issues that they raised, were examined. The results showed that, just as the response to revelations of global mass surveillance spawned new advocacy networks, the pandemic has given rise to new collaborations between technical, human rights and scientific communities, which emerged to promote and protect human rights online and offline.

In the process, some of same tensions arose as had previously been apparent in relation to human rights and the Internet. The 'appification' of the pandemic revealed tensions between centralised and decentralised systems, between privacy and the right to health, and between demands for human rights protection and regulatory approaches to technological development. These tensions echoed themes explored throughout this book about technology empowering users at the edges of the network, rather than via a single point of control, of the human rights responsibilities of the private sector, and of the duties of governments to respect, protect and promote the human rights of their peoples offline and online.

This case study illustrated how many of the conceptual and definitional challenges of the Internet and human rights have dissipated since 2010. Today, there is far greater clarity about definitions of human rights violations. There is less debate about whether human rights apply online. There is more focus on developing rights-affirming digital technologies. There are more holistic human rights analyses, with the aim of supporting public health. There has been rapid adoption, by some states at least, of modern, fit-for-purpose laws that affirm and protect human rights online and offline and, in doing so, also promote and protect public health. Even in the midst of despair about the pandemic, there has been progress.

This progress should not be overstated, since, at the same time, deep concerns remain about over-collection of personal information and intrusive surveillance. In South Korea, for example, concerns have been raised about excessive data collection and disclosure of personal data during epidemiological investigations and contact tracing, and the use of electronic bracelets on violators of self-quarantine rules.[1] Even in the midst of the pandemic, there have been prospects and challenges for human rights online; marking both progress and a sharp reminder of the limits of technology, and the need to ensure protection and promotion of human rights online *and* offline, rather than simply reaching for the 'technology solution'.

With such salutary lessons fresh in the mind, Chapter 8 turned to the new field of machine learning and artificial intelligence (AI), to see whether human rights in the digital age had some application and use in this context. These technologies are creating new social, legal and other tensions between both the benefits and opportunities and the threats and risks they pose. The field of AI is moving rapidly, creating new fault lines for human rights in the digital age.

There are some clear differences between the human rights implications of AI and those of the Internet. Compared to the Internet, for example, there would seem to be broader agreement that the starting point for AI is the fear of potential harm, whereas for the Internet the starting point was less one of fear and more one of freedom. The result has been that human rights discussions of machine learning tools have tended to focus on discrimination, bias and lack of due process, whereas the equivalent discussions in relation to Internet have focussed on freedom of expression and the right to Internet access.

But there are also similarities between the conditions and strategies which led to the emergence of human rights online, and those which are

1 B. OH, Y. CHANG and S. JEONG, 'Covid-19 and the Right to Privacy and Analysis of South Korean Experiences', JinboNet, 2019 <https://act.jinbo.net/wp/43672/> accessed 19.12.2020.

leading to the emergence of human rights in the field of AI. There is the importance of expert and community collaborations between engineers, researchers, developers, academics, ethicists, technology workers and human rights defenders. There is the need for rigorous conceptual analyses to understand how the design and use of AI and related technologies can result in human rights violations. There are the multiple stakeholders and duty-bearers across development and production lines, and the clash between private and public law and rights.

Unlike the early approach to human rights and the Internet, the international human rights bodies and UN agencies are providing a much clearer, more direct and explicit foundation for general and specific human rights analyses of AI, including regulatory responses and remedies. The UN has developed new offices with a specific focus on the application of these new forms of technology, such as the Centre for Artificial Intelligence and Robotics,[2] and inter-agency initiatives to harness AI tools in order to achieve sustainable development goals.[3] The Human Rights Council is already considering the issues brought to it by the previous Special Rapporteur on Freedom of Opinion and Expression, David Kaye.

Building, perhaps, on the foundation of advocacy for human rights online, the field of AI and human rights is developing much more quickly than its predecessor: there is little debate that human rights apply, and more concern about new and diverse forms of harm. There has also been innovation in relation to remedies, such as the proposed right to reasonable inferences. The struggle to respect and protect human rights in AI has already led to new social movements, new regulatory approaches, new expressions of human rights and new human rights defenders.

3. IMPLICATIONS

I wrote, in the Introduction, that this book was for anyone curious about the Internet, human rights and the world around them. With the increasing pace of change, and a global pandemic, feelings of fatigue can easily set in. Being curious can feel like a luxury. The complex, frustrating, messy

---

2 For more information, see: <http://www.unicri.it/in_focus/on/UNICRI_Centre_Artificial_Robotics> accessed 12.03.2021.

3 See, e.g. International Telecommunication Union <https://aiforgood.itu.int/> accessed 01.02.2021.

reality of the Internet and human rights, of human rights online, can be overwhelming.

The good news is that, today, while the field of human rights online covers vast terrain, there are more and more incredible experts ready to help aid people's understanding and engagement with the issues that are important to them.[4] From techniques to protect privacy and freedom of expression in the digital age, to technologies that enable business continuity in times of emergency and help people to work safely from home during a pandemic, to movements to combat contact tracing apps which intrude on privacy, to an algorithmic justice league: collective action is greater than sum of its parts.

Of course, technology still has significant limitations: there is no technological solution to the Covid-19 pandemic, no general artificial intelligence, and significant human rights concerns have arisen about narrow AI tools that control and manipulate social media platforms. In this book, I have attempted to show that the struggle to respond to these limitations is gradually getting easier because of the foundations laid with the struggles for access to knowledge, from communications rights, to Internet rights, to human rights online and human rights in the digital age.

The discourse about human rights online did not emerge in the international human rights system by chance. Instead, as I have also attempted to show, it was the result of collective, strategic advocacy and action. Extraordinary results can be achieved when humans work collaboratively, using human rights standards alongside technical protocols and processes to create rights-affirming technologies.

While there were deep conceptual challenges to overcome in order to progress human rights online, the work to do so is now bearing fruit in the speed of human rights analyses of new technologies. The quality and depth of this public debate about human rights online is heartening. No longer are the choices between privacy and security, privacy and health, or health and economic well-being. Instead, there is increasing awareness that security can be protected when privacy is respected, health can be protected with privacy-respecting technologies, and that the promotion of public health is necessary for long-term economic well-being.

---

4 See, e.g. D. KAYE, *Speech Police: The Global Struggle to Govern the Internet*, Columbia Global Reports, New York 2019; S. ZUBOFF, *The Age of Surveillance Capitalism: The Fight for a Human Future at the New Frontier of Power*, Profile Books, New York 2019.

Progress is sometimes fast, sometimes slow. While there were just a handful of UN Human Rights Council resolutions about the Internet in 2010, the UN General Assembly passed ten resolutions about the Internet in one 2019 session alone.[5] There are new human rights-monitoring methodologies to help document human rights violations, such as Rebecca MacKinnon's 'Ranking Digital Rights Corporate Accountability Index', which ranks the human rights performance of 24 Internet and mobile ecosystem companies from around the globe across 35 indicators.[6] Transparency reporting has risen, fallen, and risen again as companies such as Google and Twitter have tested new ways to respond to calls for them to be publicly accountable for the human rights effects of their practices, such as their engagement with law enforcement agencies.[7] 'Privacy by Design' emerged as a new field of digital rights protection, led by Professor Ann Cavoukian, and based on the idea that technology development within companies should respect and protect privacy from the very inception.[8] I am confident that other rights-affirming initiatives will emerge even though I do not yet know what these will be.

4. OUTLOOK

New technologies will continue to develop at a rapid pace. All have some human rights implications. Rather than shying away, or approaching these with fear, I would encourage a more open stance – a willingness to engage and to learn – because not only can each of us help to shape these new technologies, these incredible new technologies will also help to transform our lives.

For example, earlier in this book, I mentioned the conceptual challenge of the Internet as a space, not simply a tool: the Internet was the garden,

---

5 D. BROWN, 'UN Adopts Record Number of Resolutions about Internet Governance and Policy: Mixed Outcomes for Human Rights Online', Association for Progressive Communications, 10.01.2019 <https://www.apc.org/en/news/un-general-assembly-adopts-record-number-resolutions-internet-governance-and-policy-mixed> accessed 19.09.2020.

6 R. MACKINNON, '2019 Ranking Digital Rights Corporate Accountability Index', May 2019 <http://www.rankingdigitalrights.org> accessed 28.07.2020.

7 A. CAVOUKIAN, 'Privacy by Design: The 7 Foundational Principles' (2009) <https://www.ipc.on.ca/wp-content/uploads/Resources/7foundationalprinciples.pdf> accessed 19.09.2020.

8 See, e.g. A. RACHOVITSA, 'Engineering and Lawyering Privacy by Design: Understanding Online Privacy as both a Technical and Human Rights Issue' (2016) *International Journal of Law and Information Technology*, 24(4) 374.

conceptualised as a space where we lived, worked and played, albeit a two-dimensional space. Today, the three-dimensional spatial Internet is already upon us. The spatial Internet, or spatial Web, is a unique combination of three-dimensional physical, digital and biological, virtual and real spaces accessed via augmented or virtual reality technologies and wearable devices. Imagine being able to walk your local streets and see an entirely different virtual world mapped onto the footpaths and buildings you would usually walk by. Perhaps the same streets as they were centuries ago, or how they will look in fifty years if the effects of climate change continue. The spatial Internet will be a new kind of place, bringing together online and offline lives. It is already creating entirely new networks, made up of connections between places, people and objects, as well as their online equivalents or alternates.[9]

The 'spatial Internet', 'spatial Web' or 'Web 3.0' – there is no single agreed definition in this emerging area. These terms might refer not only to the spatially enabled World Wide Web, but also to the set of open geospatial resources (such as published data or related services) available to help people publish, find and use geospatial information. Building this new spatial Web will need technological infrastructure, including wearable devices, distributed computing (enabled by 5G and AI technologies) and distributed ledger technology (such as blockchain). To be effective, this infrastructure will need to be interoperable, which means it will need to be designed to work together.

This will bring human rights challenges: some new, some along old fault lines of power, privilege and access to knowledge. There are so many questions. Who will decide the rules – the protocols – for engineering or designing the standards that will apply in these new spaces? Will the processes for developing these protocols be multi-stakeholder and collaborative, or will they be proprietary, monopolised and closed to public access?

Just as we saw with the technical community's approach of multi-stakeholder development of open protocols and standards for the Internet, communities are already developing open, shared standards for the spatial Internet. The World Wide Web Consortium (W3C) led by Tim Berners-Lee, the inventor of Internet Protocols, and standards for URLs and

---

9 For a useful overview see G. RENÉ and D. MAPES, 'The Spatial Web: How Web 3.0 will Connect Humans, Machines and AI to Transform the World', Medium, 03.10.2019 <https://www.medium.com/swlh/an-introduction-to-the-spatial-web-bb8127f9ac45> accessed 07.03.2021.

HTTP, discussed in Chapter 1, continues to help develop open standards and Protocols in relation to the publication of spatial data on the Web, and the use of technologies as they might apply to location.[10] Another such community is the Open Geospatial Consortium, which has more than 500 technical, business, government and academic organisations, all cooperating with the aim of making geospatial local information findable, accessible, interoperable and reusable.[11] There is also a strong push to ensure that new standards enable interoperability that aligns with decentralised and democratic participation principles, including the work of the Institute of Electrical and Electronics Engineers, the Spatial Web Foundation, and Open AR Cloud.[12]

Ethical and human rights issues are already emerging. For example, it is possible to licence rights to the exterior of a building as virtual real estate for use in spatial Internet products. What are the implications of this new market? Will its participants reflect the inequitable distribution of existing land ownership and wealth, or will there be new opportunities to close such gaps? Could a spatial Web alter our sense of reality and, if so, what ethical issues does this raise for developers, engineers and data stewards, and how will they navigate these?

How will human rights such as privacy, non-discrimination and freedom of association apply in these new spaces, and how will these rights be protected in their design and creation? What kinds of human rights violations might occur, who will be accountable for these, and what kinds of remedies would be appropriate or meaningful for a human rights violation and the new types of harms that occur in these new spaces?

New collaborations will emerge to respond to these questions. Architects and artists, for example, may be at the forefront of seeing the human rights implications of designing and building these new spaces. Geographers, archaeologists and historians will have a critical role to play in mapping and revealing the cultural, social and political issues that emerge in the choices made about the development and creation of these new spaces, and their inevitable human rights implications. My experience with human rights and the Internet, and human rights in the digital age, tells me that these kinds of collaborations are critical and, once formed,

---

10 See Chapter 1. See also, e.g. J. TANDY, L. VAN DEN BRINK and P. BARNAGHI (eds.), 'Spatial Data on the Web: Best Practices', W3C Working Group Note 28.09.17 <https://www.w3.org/TR/sdw-bp/> accessed 22.12.2020.

11 The Geospatial Consortium <https://www.ogc.org/about> accessed 22.12.2020.

12 Open Augmented Reality Cloud <https://www.openarcloud.org/> 22.12.2020.

can create stronger human rights affirming policy and practice. In light of this, and despite occasional feelings of despair, I remain optimistic.

The remarkable successes of the Internet and human rights communities were not achieved by chance. We do not know whether human rights online and human rights in the digital age, like communication rights and Internet rights, will fade away and become redundant, or develop into something stronger as other technologies develop. But we can all play a part in the continuing struggle to promote and protect our human rights online and offline in the digital age.

INDEX

ABOUT THE AUTHOR

Joy Liddicoat (LLM) specialises in human rights, privacy and technology law. A former Human Rights Commissioner and Assistant Privacy Commissioner, Joy is Vice President of InternetNZ, responsible for the country code top level domain .nz. She has represented government, technical community and civil society organisations at national and international levels, including as an Internet Rights Specialist for the Association for Progressive Communications and at the International Corporation for Assigned Names and Numbers, ICANN. Joy lives in New Zealand and is a research affiliate with the Law Faculty at the University of Otago.

www.ingramcontent.com/pod-product-compliance
Ingram Content Group UK Ltd.
Pitfield, Milton Keynes, MK11 3LW, UK
UKHW021012120926
8556IPUK00039B/1033

9 781839 700590